AccountingPy

AccountingPy
PYTHON FOR ACCOUNTANTS

A practical guide for accounting industry professionals to adopt
Python as a general purpose programming language in their work

by JARED SELF

First Edition

AccountingPy

Python For Accountants

ISBN   979-8-9889917-9-3 *Paperback*

Contents

Preface

THE NEED FOR AN ACCOUNTANT TO PROGRAM

In the early 2010s, I worked as an outsourced controller for several companies through a CFO consulting firm. One of my clients was a leather goods manufacturer and DTC (Direct To Consumer) eCommerce brand. Their business model was complex, dealing with every aspect of the product, from raw goods, assembly, distribution, social media marketing, brand awareness, and web design.

Although early in my career, I had already earned a strong reputation as a QuickBooks and manufacturing software specialist. Not only was I the company's controller, but I also managed almost all aspects of accounting procedures. Since the manufacturing company had an extensive range of products, including various colors, styles, and accessories, data management and analysis became challenging due to the thousands of items involved.

I often spent several hours transferring data from one platform to another, relying on Excel and other available tools. While I had proficiency for my level of experience, some of the software programs proved to be a challenge. I remember sitting in a meeting with the CEO and COO one afternoon. They were looking for a specific metric. The data I needed to present that metric was inside the software we were using (I could see it in the User Interface), but I couldn't access it through the native reports. As a result, I couldn't give them the metrics. This encounter made me realize the need to upgrade my data processing and automation skills.

As a result, I followed the path taken by numerous accountants before me. I learned VBA (back when Power-Query was still a novelty). As time progressed, I developed my VBA skills considerably. I eventually reached a level where I could create personalized Access databases and utilize VBA to execute API calls. My career had also progressed and I was employed by one of Utah's most successful Kickstarter brands. While there, I was given a task that involved gathering customer and order information from approximately ten different sources. During the analysis, I exceeded Access's 2GB threshold and had an additional 4GB of data to process for the project. VBA also became quite a problem as I pushed its limits. Ultimately, I failed to achieve my objectives with VBA. Late one night (or rather, early the next morning), while attempting to solve the issue, I ultimately accepted that VBA, Access, and Excel were inadequate by themselves for modern accounting requirements. I'm not suggesting we abandon Excel, I'm just suggesting it's not enough by itself.

So now the question is "what technology should modern accountants learn to meet the demand of today's tech stack." Although many accounting tools are available, almost every company I worked for had unique problems that commercial software didn't solve. This shouldn't be news to any accountants. It's a fact that accountants have been aware of for some time. In fact, it's why accountants excelled at using Excel. Since the advent of the office computer, accountants have used spreadsheet software to build unique solutions for their challenges. But as technology improved, so did the demand for more sophisticated and technical solutions.

Historically, accountants have been reliant on software developers to create solutions where spreadsheet software falls short. That said, have you ever said to yourself "those developers never spoke to an accountant before they built that". I know I have. What's worse is when management demands we use that software. I firmly believe that our industry should create our own solutions. If you're reading this book, you may have already come to the same realization. Since accountants know best what accountants need, it's time for Accountants to embrace a general programming language as our own and begin building our own solutions.

SELECTING A PROGRAMMING LANGUAGE TO ADOPT

The primary issue at hand is selecting a programming language that is suitable for our profession. VBA has been extensively utilized by many accountants over the years. So should it be a similar language like VB.net? If not VB.net maybe it's cousin C# (both maintained by Microsoft)? Another option could be Javascript, which is the programming language of the internet. How about C++? Initially, I was unsure which one to adopt, so I delved into the fundamentals of each language. Although each has its own strengths, there are significant disadvantages to many of them that cannot be overlooked. Consequently, I decided to identify the key aspects that a programming language must possess for it to be adopted by the accounting industry. Below is my subjective assessment of the major programming languages currently available that should be considered.

	Easy To Learn	Open Source	Easy Desktop Apps	OOP & Script	Data Focus	General Purpose Language	Sticking Around
VBA	X	X	X	X			
VB.Net		X	X			X	
C#		X	X			X	X
JavaScript	X	X		X		X	X
C							X
Java		X				X	X
Ruby	X	X			X		
R		X		X	X		X
C++			X	X	X		X
SQL	X	X		X	X		X
Python	X	X	X	X	X	X	X

From my analysis, Python is the best suited programming language for the accounting industry. Below are some justifications.

- Python is relatively easy to learn, and accountants can easily leverage their knowledge of spreadsheet software while learning Python.
- Python is an open-source language, making it accessible to those who may not have the budget for extra software.
- Python is relatively easy to use in developing desktop applications, especially in Windows environments.
- Python supports both scripts and object-oriented programming, making it a versatile language.
- The Data Science industry has already embraced Python, and its focus on data makes it an excellent option for accountants as well.
- Python is a general-purpose language, meaning that it can be used in various environments, including Windows, Android, Mac, and Linux.
- Python is expected to remain relevant for some time, which is crucial for accountants who cannot afford to invest in languages that are likely to become outdated soon.
- Python plays nice with other software. Although I didn't include this in the grid, it was one of the criteria. The worst thing about VBA is it doesn't play nice with other types of data like JSON.

Now that I had selected the programming language, I thought the problem-solving process would be straight-forward. However, it wasn't that simple for me. Although Python was the obvious choice, there was very little training specifically directed towards accountants. I had to sift through numerous data science and web development courses and found only a small percentage of the material to be relevant. Additionally, I even resorted to hiring programmers to tutor me and help solve complex issues that were not covered in other courses. I had to exhaust every possible avenue since there wasn't a clear path for me to follow. Even though I gained a lot of knowledge about Python and its capabilities, I knew only a few accountants could invest the time I did in learning the language. So I have written this book to assist future accountants who may find themselves in a similar predicament as I was in.

This book represents the culmination of years of struggle and learning, condensed into a single volume. My objective is to provide a clear path for accountants to create successful programs without having to delve into the intricate complexities of Python (as I had to). By reading this book, you can potentially learn in a matter of weeks or months what took me years of trial and error.

Supplemental to this book is a package of code that can be found at *https://accountingpy.com/downloads*. Download the code so you can have working examples to refer to. Also consider following me on LinkedIn (*https://www.linkedin.com/in/jared-self/*) where I try to post regularly about projects I'm working on and updates to things like this book. I appreciate your support in purchasing this book. I hope you like it and it inspires you to become your accounting department's tech hero.

Sincerely,
Jared Self

SECTION 1

BASICS

CHAPTER 1

Basic Development Tools

THONNY (A SIMPLE BEGINNERS IDE)

Python has versions. This is something you need to be aware of and pay attention to. There are also different IDE's (Integrated Development Environment) to choose from. Choosing an IDE is kind of like choosing a spreadsheet software. You may use Microsoft Excel or Google Sheets. They are essentially the same but also vastly different. It's important to learn about versions and environments at some point. However, right now it may be better to consider versions as similar to updates in QuickBooks Desktop.

If you create a company file in QuickBooks Desktop 2021 you shouldn't try to open it with QuickBooks Desktop 2020. QuickBooks won't let you open the newer file with an older version. Python will let you run newer code in an older version. You'll just come across errors. You also don't want to open a company file created in QuickBooks Desktop 2005 with QuickBooks Desktop 2021. Just like that, running older code with newer versions of Python can also create problems. The ideal solution is to run your code with the same version it was developed with.

Initially, we will use a simple IDE called Thonny (*https://thonny.org/*). Please don't get too attached to the editor because we'll eventually switch to Pycharm. I use Thonny because it will handle environment and Python versions automatically. That allows us to focus on just learning Python. I'm using Thonny 4.0.1 with Python 3.10.6 pre-installed for this book. Feel free to use any version of Python or Thonny newer than this.

For this book, I'll use windows and reference how to do things in windows. More power to you if you're using a MAC (or Unix), but you'll need to convert the instructions into your operating system's equivalent.

The installation executable can be downloaded at *https://thonny.org* as the first step. The link to download the Thonny executable will appear when you hover your mouse over the name of your OS. When you double-click the program after downloading it, it will install. From there, you can access Thonny from the "Start" menu. Additional information is provided in figure 1.1.

Thonny

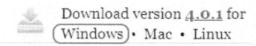

Download version 4.0.1 for (Windows) · Mac · Linux

Official downloads for Windows

Installer with 64-bit Python 3.10, requires 64-bit Windows 8.1 / 10 / 11
thonny-4.0.1.exe (20.4 MB) ⇐ *recommended for you*

Installer with 32-bit Python 3.8, suitable for all Windows versions since 7
thonny-py38-4.0.1.exe (18.9 MB)

NB! The installers have been signed with a new certificate which hasn't built
up its reputation yet. You may need to click through your browser warning
(e.g. choose "Keep" instead of "Discard" in Chrome) and Windows Defender
warning (More info ⇒ Run anyway).

Portable variant with 64-bit Python 3.10
thonny-4.0.1-windows-portable.zip (30.5 MB)

Portable variant with 32-bit Python 3.8
thonny-py38-4.0.1-windows-portable.zip (28.6 MB)

Re-using an existing Python installation (for advanced users)
`pip install thonny`

Figure 1.1

Now let's do some setup of Thonny so we're both looking at the same thing. In view, I suggest selecting only the following options: Files, Object Inspector, Shell, and Variables.

At first the page that is open will say <untitled>. We want to save our work so let's go ahead and save our first project file.

1. Go to File > Save As
2. Choose Documents to put your folders in
3. Create a new folder named PythonProjects
4. Under PythonProjects, create a folder named AccountingPy
5. Under AccountingPy, create a folder named Chapter1
6. Name this file "hello_world" (the ending of ".py" will be created automatically)

 Note: Usually, you don't want to add numbers in the names of your files and especially as the first letters of your file. We're going to break that rule for the sake of education (so don't get attached to it).

Inside the first line of the page add the following code:

```
print('Hello World!')
```

Now press F5 or the green circle with the white arrow to run the program (see figure 1.2)

Figure 1.2

Congratulations, you've run your first program! You printed out onto the shell the text "Hello World!". Traditionally, this is always the first thing any programmer learns. The tradition is so strong I couldn't help making it our first task.

HOW PYTHON RUNS (LOW VS HIGH LEVEL LANGUAGES)

In this section, we'll delve into some technical details, but I'll do my best to ensure you can easily grasp these essential concepts. Python is not a standalone language; rather, it's a high-level programming language. You might be wondering what that means. At the core, computer code consists of binary data, i.e., 1's and 0's, which are the only two values computers truly understand. For those interested in the technicalities, specific combinations of 1's and 0's can be translated into text. Early programmers devised methods to transform sequences of text (words) into binary data, allowing them to perform mathematical operations. The process of converting human-readable text into computer code (1's and 0's) is referred to as "interpretation." Computers use "interpreters" to translate programming languages like Python into executable code.

Over time, programming languages like "C" (among other foundational languages, without delving too deep into the details) were developed as a collection of rules that had to be adhered to for computers to interpret commands. C is regarded as a low-level language. Higher-level languages are built upon lower-level languages as their foundation. For instance, to print "Hello, World!" in C, the code would appear as follows:

```
#include <stdio.h>
int main() {
    // printf() displays the string inside quotation
    printf("Hello, World!");
    return 0;
}
```

Writing such lengthy code just to print a message on the console can be tedious. Consequently, after a few layers of abstraction, Python simplifies this task by using the keyword "print." Behind the scenes, Python translates "print" into a lower-level language like C (though this might not be entirely accurate, bear with me). Subsequently, C converts its code into binary data (1's and 0's), which the computer reads and executes according to the given instructions. This is why C is classified as a low-level language, as it is closely related to the binary level. Higher-level languages are built on top of lower-level languages and are further removed from binary data. Thus, Python is essentially a combination of lower-level languages consolidated with new, more user-friendly rules, making it easier for humans to read but not as straightforward for computers to interpret.

This is not necessarily a drawback. Ultimately, humans are the ones who utilize computers, so it can be argued that programming languages should prioritize human readability over computer readability. As you progress on your Python journey, it's essential to be conscious of the underlying processes. We'll revisit this topic later; for now, simply grasp the concept that programming languages have layers, and you're working with a higher-level language in Python.

EXTREMELY BASIC CONCEPT OF OBJECTS IN PYTHON

As the title suggests, we won't delve into the intricacies in this section. The primary point to note is that objects possess two main components: they are something, and they do something. These components are referred to as attributes (representing properties) and methods (representing actions). To access an object's attribute, you employ the syntax "object_name.attribute_name".

For instance, if the object is a BalanceSheet, you might use "balance_sheet.is_balanced" to check if your balance sheet is balanced. The "is_balanced" part is the attribute. You "drilled down" to that attribute by starting with the name "balance_sheet" (which is the name of the object in this hypothetical scenario). Then, you used a period (".") to indicate that you're drilling down, followed by the attribute name "is_balanced". So, the BalanceSheet is something, in this case, represented by the "is_balanced" attribute.

Next, we might want the BalanceSheet to perform an action. For this, we use methods. Suppose we want the balance sheet to collapse all parent accounts. We can create a method named "collapse" and call it with the statement "balance_sheet.collapse()". Notice the parentheses at the end. You can identify a method by the syntax: object_name, period ("."), method_name, and parentheses "()". Sometimes, you'll add arguments to the parentheses, like "balance_sheet.collapse(lowest_accounts_only=True)".

As we progress, all of this will be explained in greater detail. However, I wanted to provide a fundamental explanation at the outset. This will help you understand when to add parentheses in your code, when to use periods, and allow you to distinguish between attributes and methods.

 Note: Functions are like methods without the objects.

CODE BLOCKS

Now, let's discuss syntax, specifically indentation. In many programming languages, a tab (indent) might not carry any significance. However, in Python, it is not only meaningful but also mandatory. Python relies on indentation to organize code. When there's an indent in the code, it is generally because it's considered "under" the code above it that isn't indented (or one indent level in from the current code). All code at the same indentation level is considered a block of code. Consider the following pseudocode:

```
statement #Code block 1 begins
if condition: #Code block 1 continues
    if condition: #Code block 2 begins
        statement #Code block 3 begins if condition is True
    else: #Code block 2 continues if condition is False
        statement #Code block 3 begins if condition is False
        statement #Code block 2 continues after block 2 if statement
statement #Code block 1 continues after block 1 if statement
```

A statement instructs the computer to perform a specific action. As we progress through the book, we'll delve deeper into how statements should be constructed and placed within your code.

AUTO COMPLETE

Most development environments come equipped with an auto-complete feature. This functionality enables you to explore objects more efficiently. While it might not seem particularly relevant to you at the moment, there will come a time when you feel frustrated or unsure about what to do with a specific line of code. When that frustration arises, remember to take advantage of this handy feature offered by your development tool.

When you begin typing in Thonny, pressing Ctrl + Spacebar will activate the auto-complete IntelliSense feature. This tool assists you in determining the available options for the object you're working with. In Figure 1.3, notice how this trick is employed after typing the period, displaying the available options for the object.

```
>>> str('sometext').|
```

```
capitalize()        capitalize() -> str
casefold(
center(             Return a capitalized version of the string.
count(
encode(             More specifically, make the first character
endswith(           have upper case and the rest lower
expandtabs(         case.
find(
format(
format_map(
```

Figure 1.3

THE COMMAND LINE

There are numerous resources available on how to navigate the command line. Here, I will teach you a few basic commands that you will likely use most often:

1. "cd" — Changes the current directory to the specified directory. Example: cd C:\Windows\System32 will change the current directory to the System32 folder in the Windows directory.
2. "cd .." — Changes the current directory back one folder. Example: cd .. while in C:\Windows\System32 will change the current directory back to C:\Windows. Notice there is a space between cd and the dots.
3. "dir" — Displays a list of files and directories in the current directory. Example: dir will show the contents of the current directory.
4. "python" — Enters a Python shell. If you use python file_location like python C:\Users\selfjared\script_to_run.py, it will run the specified Python script. To exit the Python shell, use exit(). Note that when you use the python command, you're using the default Python version specified in the PATH of your System Environment Variables. If you have only one Python version installed, you should be fine. If you have multiple versions, you may need to make some changes to your System Environment Variables. To determine the default version, use the command python --version. If you're using Thonny, this won't be an issue for the short term.

As we progress through the book, we will discuss environments and their management in more detail. At this stage, the aim is to make you aware of the concept so that you have a foundational understanding moving forward.

CHAPTER 2

Basic Data Types

Since this course is tailored for accountants rather than computer scientists, we won't delve too deeply into data types. Our focus is on practical application and covering essential information that you need to know to start using Python effectively. With that in mind, let's discuss some basic concepts to lay the foundation for further learning and application.

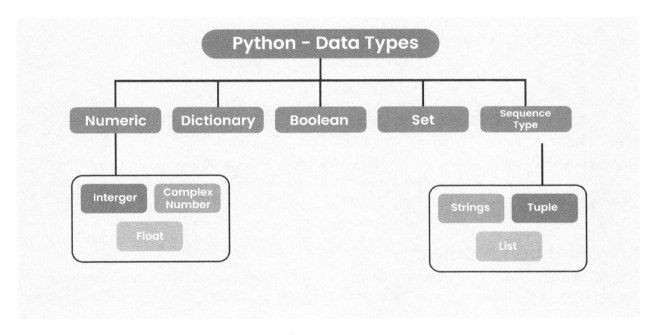

There are 4 basic data types your really need to know:

- Integers
- Floating-Point Numbers
- Boolean ("Truthiness")
- Strings

```
1  import sys
2  print('size of integer :--> ', sys.getsizeof(int()))
3  print('size of float:--> ', sys.getsizeof(float()))
4  print('size of string :--> ', sys.getsizeof(str()))
5  print('size of list :--> ', sys.getsizeof(list()))
6  print('size of set :--> ', sys.getsizeof(set()))
7  print('size of tuple :--> ', sys.getsizeof(tuple()))
8  print('size of dictitonary :--> ', sys.getsizeof(dict()))
```

Shell ×

```
>>> %Run -c $EDITOR_CONTENT
  size of integer :-->  24
  size of float:-->  24
  size of string :-->   49
  size of list :-->  56
  size of set :-->  216
  size of tuple :-->   40
  size of dictitonary :-->   64
```

INTEGERS

Integers are whole numbers without a decimal point and can be either positive or negative. Examples include -3, -2, -1, 0, 1, 2, and 3. They are a basic data type in Python and can be used in various mathematical operations and calculations.

FLOATING-POINT NUMBERS

Floating-point numbers (float) are similar to integers, but they include decimal points. Floats can also be either positive or negative. While integers and decimal numbers can coexist within the same cell in spreadsheets, they are treated as distinct data types in Python.

It's important to note that if you add a decimal number to an integer in Python, the result will be a floating-point number. Keep this in mind as you work with numerical data in your Python scripts.

PRACTICE INTEGERS AND FLOATS

Let's do some examples before we get to strings. In Thonny create a new folder under AccountingPy named Chapter2. Then create a new document by the shortcut Ctrl + N or File > New. Then save the file with the name "python_numbers_and_bool". Type the following code into the file:

```
revenue = 1000
cogs = 430
```

```
admin_expenses = 30
payroll = 103
advertising= 250
interest_expense = 20

gross_margin = revenue - cogs
print(gross_margin)

ebitda = gross_margin - admin_expenses - payroll - advertising
print(ebitda)

net_income = ebitda — interest_expense
print(net_income)
```

If you click on run, your output should look something like figure figure 2.1

```
Shell

>>> %Run numbers_and_bool.py
    570
    187
    167

>>>
```

Figure 2.1

VARIABLES

Now, let's analyze what happened. When you hit run, Python starts at the top of the page and executes lines of code from top to bottom. In this example, the first action was to create a "variable" named "revenue" and assign it the value of 1000. When assigning variables, the variable name is always on the left side of a single equals sign. Now, instead of remembering the number 1000 for the rest of the code, Python knows it should replace the word "revenue" with the integer value of 1000.

Here are the rules for declaring a Python variable:

- A variable name must start with a letter or the underscore character.
- A variable name cannot start with a number.
- A variable name can only contain alphanumeric characters and underscores (A-z, 0-9, and _).
- Variable names are case-sensitive (age, Age, and AGE are three different variables).

 Note: Additionally, avoid using any of the following characters in your variable names, as they are all reserved for different types of operations in Python:

`:'"",<>/?|\()!@#$%^&*~-+`

23

False	class	finally	is	return
None	continue	for	lambda	try
True	def	from	nonlocal	while
and	del	global	not	with
as	elif	if	or	yield
assert	else	import	pass	
break	except			

You'll also want to be cautious with characters that can be easily confused, such as O vs zero (o) or l (L) vs one (1). Context matters when choosing variable names. For example, later in the book, we'll use the name pl_2024. As an accountant, you'll recognize this as Profit and Loss for 2024. Because context clarifies this variable's name, it's acceptable to bend some of the best practices.

When declaring variables in Python, you'll want to use what's called snake_case (a nod to Python being a snake) for the variable name. This means using all lowercase characters with underscores ("_") between words. Additionally, it's a good practice to avoid using numbers in your variable names and to use singular or plural words as appropriate. We'll discuss lists and similar data structures later, but if you have multiple invoices in a variable, name it "invoices" instead of "invoice".

Good examples: invoice, invoices, vendor_invoice, cogs, net_income
Bad examples: Cogs, Cost_of_goods_sold, invoice_01, 01_Invoice, MyInvoice

Another aspect to consider is the variable name itself. When writing your code, choose names that are descriptive. Don't be afraid to use longer, more descriptive names. It's much better to type a longer name than to try to decipher a cryptic naming convention you came up with two years ago. Ask yourself, "If another accountant were to review this code and try to edit it, could they understand what that variable is just by reading the name?" If the answer is no, consider changing the name to something more descriptive.

Good Example / Bad Example:
net_income_percentage / net
refresh_token_expires_in_seconds / expires
pl_prior_year_dict / prior_year (dict is a well-established Python acronym for dictionary)

If you followed my earlier instructions, you should also be able to see the Variables window (View > Variables). The Variables window should look something like Figure 1.4.

Variables	
Name	Value
admin_expenses	30
advertising	250
cogs	430
ebitda	187
gross_margin	570
interest_expense	20
net_income	167
payroll	103
revenue	1000

Figure 2.2

Observe in Figure 2.2 that there are several variables, each with their own value. After running a script like this, Thonny keeps the shell open with variables in memory, meaning the program is still running. If you go to the shell and type in the name of a variable, such as "gross_margin", it will return the number 570, as shown in Figure 2.3.

```
Shell

>>> %Run numbers_and_bool.py
  570
  187
  167
>>> gross_margin
570
>>> |
```

Figure 2.3

There is also information in the Object Inspector, but we'll revisit that later. To stop the program, press the red stop sign, use the keyboard shortcut Ctrl+F2, or select Run > Stop/Restart Backend from the menu.

PRACTICE BASIC MATH

At this point, we want to focus on practicing some math in Python, so go ahead and run the program again to load all of those variables into memory for us to use.

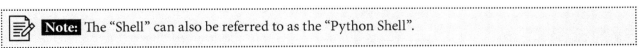

Note: The "Shell" can also be referred to as the "Python Shell".

In the shell, let's perform some simple math. Addition, subtraction, multiplication, and division all follow the same general syntax as spreadsheet formulas, with the exception that you don't put an equal sign ("=") in front. Type the following lines in the shell one at a time, pressing enter after each line to see the returned value:

```
advertising + cogs
```

Should return 680

```
revenue — advertising + cogs
```

Should return 1180

```
revenue — (advertising + cogs)
```

Should return 320. Notice the order of operations applies here. As an accountant, and spreadsheet user already, this should feel familiar.

```
gross_margin / revenue
```

Should return 0.57

```
gross_margin_percentage = gross_margin / revenue
net_income_percentage = net_income / revenue
```

Shouldn't return anything, but notice it adds the gross_margine_percentage and net_income_percentage variables to memory (0.57 and 0.167 respectively).

```
gross_margin_percentage * 2000
```

Notice 1140.0 as a float is returned instead of an integer. It's because one of the numbers in the equation was a float so the returned value will be a float.

VARIABLE TYPES

At this point, you may have noticed that we didn't have to declare any variable types. If you've experimented with VBA or other programming languages, you might have encountered the need to identify a variable and its type before using it. In Python, you don't have to declare variable types because they undergo implicit conversion. You don't need to memorize the term, but you should be aware that the type is determined during runtime. As a result, a variable can change from an integer to a float and then to a string, all without declaring its value type beforehand (although, it's not recommended to make all of these changes in the same script). Consequently, it's helpful to use the "type" function at times to determine a variable's type.

Back in the shell, you can use the following code to determine a variable's type:

```
type(cogs)
```

Should return <class 'int'>

If you want to print out the type of a variable inside the program, you'll want to nest the type() function inside the print() function. If you're familiar with spreadsheets, you should already be comfortable with the concept of nesting functions. Here's an example of how to do this in Python:

```
print(type(0.167))
```

Should return <class 'float'>

When you run this line of code, it will print the type of 0.167 to the console. In this case, it would print <class 'float'>, indicating that 0.167 is of the float type.

BOOLEAN ("TRUTHINESS")

Boolean (Bool) means True or False. In spreadsheet's you've already used "if" statements so this should be a familiar concept to you. Where Python differs is with something called "truthy" and "falsy". In Python, the concept of "truthy" and "falsy" values is used to determine whether a value is considered to be true or false in a boolean context. A "truthy" value is considered true when it is explicitly True, is not empty, is not None, or is any number other than zero (or 0.0). Conversely, a "falsy" value is considered false when it is explicitly False, is empty, is None, or is the value of 0 (zero).

This flexibility allows Python to simplify conditional statements, such as "if" statements, by evaluating values in a boolean context without explicitly checking each condition. Please note that at this point, we are only providing a brief overview of "if" statements. Our main focus is not to teach "if" statements in-depth, as that will be covered later in the course.

If you haven't done so yet, stop the program from running by clicking the stop button. After the last line of your code, let's add a few more lines. It's important to remember that the values 'True' and 'False' must be capitalized, as they are constants and not variables. See the examples below:

```
print(True)
print(False)
print(True == False) #Comparing if True is equal to False
print(True != False) #Comparing if True is not equal to False
```

 Note: When commenting on code in Python, the hash (#) symbol is used. Any text following the hash will be considered a comment, and it won't be executed or trigger a Python error message.

After adding the lines you can run the program again.

Notice the last who are comparisons. In Python if you want to compare two values you have "==" which means "is equal to" and "!=" which means "is not equal to". Now let's compare some other values and notice what the results are. Put the following code at the end of the document and run it again or enter each line in the shell one at a time. Mainly play around with what is True in Python.

```
print(True == 1) #Comparing if True is equal to the integer 1 (it is)
print(True == 1.0) #Comparing if True is equal to the float 1 (it is)
print(True == 2) #Will Return False
if 2: print('true') #Will Return True (because Truthy) and print 'true'
if -2: print('true') #Will Return True (because Truthy) and print 'true'
if 'a_random_word_str': print('true') #Is also Truthy and prints 'true'
```

Once you've added the new lines, go ahead and run the program again. Pay attention to the final comparisons. In Python, if you want to compare two values, you can use "==" (meaning "is equal to") and "!=" (meaning "is not equal to"). Now let's explore some other comparisons and observe their results. Add the following code to the end of your script and run it again, or alternatively, input each line into the Python shell one by one. The primary goal is to gain a deeper understanding of what evaluates to 'True' in Python.

```
print(False == 0) #True
print(False == 0.0) #True
print(False == None) #False because None is the absence of a value
if 0: print('true') #False and will not print
if None: print('true') #Falsy and will not print
if not None: print('true') #Truthy (because not) and will not print
```

Similar to 'True' and 'False', 'None' is also a constant, not a variable. You'll find that 'None' does not equal 'False' when compared directly. Yet, when used in an 'if' statement, 'None' yields a 'falsy' result.

If you're feeling confused, that's completely understandable, as grasping the concepts of "truthy" and "falsy" can be challenging at first. Rest assured, with practice, these ideas will become more intuitive as you work with "if" statements. For now, simply acknowledge that "truthy" and "falsy" can be peculiar, and they'll become clearer as you gain experience.

Note: One more odd thing. "True" is literally equal to the value 1, while "False" is literally equal to the value zero (0). This means that an expression like "True + True + True" evaluates to the integer 3. Although you may not typically use "True" or "False" in mathematical equations, understanding their numeric representations can provide deeper insights into their behavior.

STRINGS

Strings in Python share many similarities with strings in spreadsheets, which is one of the reasons why Python is an ideal programming language for accountants. For instance, Python uses the "len()" function to determine the number of characters in a string, just like spreadsheets. However, one difference is that Python typically employs single quotes instead of double quotes to create a string. This might take some getting used to, but it's not too difficult to adapt. Another similarity is the ability to nest a single quote within a double quote. Interestingly, Python also allows you to do the reverse by enclosing double quotes within single quotes. We can access the characters in a string in three ways:

1. Indexing: One way is to treat strings as a list and use index values.
2. Negative Indexing: Similar to a list, Python allows negative indexing for its strings.
3. Slicing: Access a range of characters in a string by using the slicing operator colon (:)

Now, let's explore some examples to demonstrate these concepts.

```python
1  greet = 'hello'
2
3  # access 1st index element (Indexing)
4  print(greet[1]) # "e"
5
6  # access 4th last element (Negative Indexing)
7  print(greet[-4]) # "e"
8
9  # access character from 1st index to 3rd index (Slicing)
10 print(greet[1:4])  # "ell"
```

Shell

```
>>> %Run -c $EDITOR_CONTENT
    e
    e
    ell
```

Create a new document named "python_strings.py". Write the following into the document:

```python
print('my_string')
print("my_string")
```

```
print("I'm happy") #Notice single quote in double
print(len("my_string")) #Will return the count of characters
customer_first_name = 'Joe'
print('Hey ' + customer_first_name + ", it's great to see you.")
```

Notice how single and double quotes are interchangeable. Even though they are, the rule is to use single quotes unless you have to use double quotes.

Here are a couple of more examples to add to the document:

```
print('first line\nsecond line') #Use \n for new line.
print("""First Line
Second Line""") #Notice formatting follows if you use 3 quotes
print('''First Line
Second Line''') #Notice formatting follows if you use 3 quotes
```

There are various methods you may use to add variables to your strings. I will demonstrate the many approaches for the benefit of your education and knowledge, but I will advise you to stick with a specific one unless it is absolutely required.

```
first_name = 'Joe'
print('Hey ' + first_name + '.')
print('Hey %s' % first_name)
print('Hey {first_name}.'.format(first_name=first_name))
print(f'Hey {first_name}.') #This is the suggested way called f-string
```

```
1  message = 'Python Strings'
2  message[0] = 'h'
3  print(message)
```

Shell ×

```
>>> %Run -c $EDITOR_CONTENT
   Traceback (most recent call last):
      File "<string>", line 2, in <module>
   TypeError: 'str' object does not support item assignment
```

Here are some methods you can use with strings:

Methods	Descriptions
upper()	converts the string to uppercase
lower()	converts the string to lowercase
partition()	returns a tuple
replace()	replaces substring inside
find()	returns the index of first occurrence of substring
rstrip()	removes trailing characters
split()	splits string from left
startswith()	checks if string starts with the specified string
isnumeric()	checks numeric characters
index()	returns index of substring

The suggested way is to use an f-string unless another method is necessary. We won't go over the exceptions in this book. To use the f-string, add the letter f before the first quote. Then add the variable in curly brackets {}.

Lists, Tuples, Sets, Dictionaries

LIST BASICS

Lists in Python are exactly what they sound like — an ordered collection of items. It's crucial to remember that lists maintain their order, unlike some other Python data structures, such as dictionaries. To create a list, all you need are square brackets [], with each item separated by commas. To practice, create a new folder called "Chapter3" under the "AccountingPy" directory, and then create another folder within it named "python_lists_basics". Inside the file add these examples:

```
empty_list = [] #This is an empty list. It's Falsy in an if statement
single_list = [2] #List with single item
numbers_list = [1, 2, 3] #List with multiple items
mixed_list = [1, 'z', 3] #Lists can hold any value as an item
print(empty_list)
print(single_list)
print(numbers_list)
print(mixed_list)
```

List of Age

Lists Elements

EXTRACT FROM LIST

Creating a list is relatively simple. But how do we extract data from lists? To do that, you need to understand indexing. You may have been conditioned to think that the first item in a list corresponds to the number one

(1), especially if you have experience with spreadsheets, where the first row is labeled as row one. However, in computer programming and Python, the first index is actually zero. When working with "arrays" (no need to memorize this term), the item in the first position is indexed as zero, followed by one, two, and so on. So, to select the third item in a list, you'll use the index number 2. Once you become familiar with this zero-based counting method, it will feel like second nature. All you need is some practice. Refer to Figure 3.1 for a visual representation of this concept.

length = 5

	'p'	'r'	'o'	'b'	'e'
index	0	1	2	3	4
negative index	-5	-4	-3	-2	-1

Figure 3.1

Let's practice with the lists we created above. Now to access a specific item, you write the variable's name. Then add brackets at the end with the index number in the bracket. Add these examples to the end of the python_lists document:

```
print(numbers_list[0]) #Should return the number 1
print(numbers_list[1]) #Should return the number 2
print(numbers_list[2]) #Should return the number 3
```

We can't use zero again when trying to index backward because it's the first position. So instead of zero, we're beginning with -1 as the far right list item. Add the following to your document:

```
print(numbers_list[-1]) #Should return the number 3
print(numbers_list[-2]) #Should return the number 2
print(numbers_list[-3]) #Should return the number 1
```

Let's say you want to make a variable equal to a list item:

```
something_from_a_list = mixed_list[1]
print(something_from_a_list) #Should print 'z'
```

NESTED LIST

Notice that items in lists can be any object. That includes other nested lists, strings, etc. For example, here is a list inside of a list to add to the document:

```
nested_list = [
    ['a', 'b', 'c'],
```

```
    [1, 2, 3]
] #A list with two items, each one a list themselves.
print(nested_list)
```

How do we extract from a list inside of a list? It's easiest to answer this when you look at the type of item. A list inside of a list is just another list. It's easiest to show this using the type function:

```
print(type(nested_list)) #As expected the type is <class 'list'>
print(type(nested_list[0])) #As expected the type is <class 'list'>
```

In this case, both the parent and the nested child are lists. While it may not seem obvious at first, it implies that "nested_list[o]" can be treated as a value in itself. If we were to draw a parallel with spreadsheets, we could consider this as =(nested_list[o]), where the parentheses separate "nested_list[o]" as its own value. So, if "nested_list[o]" is a list, how do you access the first item? You would do it the same way as you would for any list in Python—by appending brackets with the index [o] at the end. Thus, "nested_list[o][o]" would retrieve the first item from the nested list. If you're familiar with spreadsheet syntax, you might find it helpful to think of it as =(nested_list[o])[o].

However, don't get too fixated on the spreadsheet analogy. The example provided is not accurate syntax for either spreadsheets or Python. If this explanation is not clear, feel free to skip the spreadsheet example and focus on understanding the concept through the next approach I'll present.

An alternative way to grasp this idea is to assign the nested list to a variable and examine both lists like this:

```
variable_list = nested_list[0]
print(nested_list[0][0])
print(variable_list[0])
print(nested_list[0][0] == variable_list[0]) #should print True
```

SLICING

Slicing in Python is incredibly convenient, as it combines your spreadsheet's left, right, and mid functions into a simple, compact syntax. You might wonder why I'm introducing slicing, which seems like an unusual concept, in the list section. That's because every string of text in Python is essentially just a list of characters — quite a revelation, isn't it?

The syntax for slicing is as follows: list_name[start:stop:step]. Just remember "start, stop, step," and you should be good. Let's break down what each term means:

- **start:** The index of the first item to include. The default is 0.
- **stop:** The index of the first item to NOT include (the index where you should stop). The default is None (which means it will continue until the list ends).
- **step:** How many steps to take for the next character. The default is 1. If you choose 2, you will take 2 steps each time (every other) until the stop index. Although it's helpful to be aware of this feature, I've only used it once or twice while learning Python.

I particularly enjoy using slicing with SKUs. I used to be a controller for a leather manufacturing company, which had colors, types, sizes, hardware, and all kinds of attributes in their SKUs. With thousands of SKUs to work with, I would spend a considerable amount of time splitting out their SKUs to report consolidated sales figures. I didn't know Python then, but I did know some VBA. While VBA helped, it wasn't as versatile as Python.

Let's consider the SKU "COMP-BLK-LG-BK-V02". This represents a composition notebook — black leather — large size — with a buckle — version 2. For educational purposes, let's assume the dashes are always at the same location in the SKU string. So, the first dash is always at index number 4. Here's how we would split out the different attributes:

```
sku = 'COMP-BLK-LG-BK-V02'
product_code = sku[:4] #[0:4:1]
print(product_code) #prints 'COMP'
color_code = sku[5:8] #[5:8:1] start at 5th index, stops at 8th index
print(color_code) #prints 'BLK'
```

Negative numbers can be used as well. When indexing forward, you start with index zero. You can't have a negative zero; it just doesn't exist. So for practical reasons, negatives start at -1. So -1 refers to the last letter (list item), and -2 is before that. So considering the same SKU as above, see these examples:

```
version_code = sku[-3:] #[-3:None:1] start at -3rd index and don't stop
print(version_code) #prints 'V02'
sku_less_version_code = sku[:-4] #[0:-4:1] end at -4th index
#Remember the item at the stop argument index is not included
#In this example index -4 is not included
print(sku_less_version_code) #prints 'V02'

print(sku[-3:-4]) #Returns None because stop is before start
print(sku[-3:-3]) #Prints "" because stop index isn't included
print(sku[-3:-2]) #Prints "V" because it's the start position -3
```

Let's suppose that because of the rules governing my SKUs, the features (such as black, buckle, etc.) were separated by dashes, but the number of codes separating the colors and versions varied. How could we make a pseudo code containing only the product code-color code-version code? Check it out for yourself, then consider these various approaches to the same issue:

```
#solution 1
#if the positions are known
print(sku[:8] + sku[-4:])

#solution 2
#if positions are not know, this is a way you could do it
#This isn't the best way, it just is a way
product_code_dash_index = sku.index('-')
#the second argument for the index function is the start position
color_code_dash_index = sku.index('-', product_code_dash_index + 1)
#slicing two colons together reverses the order of the list.
```

```
#also notice the order of operations
version_code_negative_index =  -(str(sku[::-1]).index('-')+1)
#Notice backslash below breaks the statement into another line
truncated_sku = sku[:color_code_dash_index] \
                + sku[version_code_negative_index:]
print(truncated_sku)
```

OTHER LIST TASKS

Here are some more things you can do with lists:

```
print(numbers_list + mixed_list) #combining two lists
print(numbers_list + ['e', 4, 'word']) #combining two lists
print(numbers_list)
numbers_list.append('another_thing') #add to end of list
print(numbers_list)
print(numbers_list + ['that_thing']) #add to end of list
print(numbers_list)
removed_first = numbers_list.pop(0) #remove first item from list
removed_last = numbers_list.pop(-1) #remove last item from list
print(removed_first)
print(removed_last)
print(numbers_list)
print(len(numbers_list)) #to get the length of a list
```

LIST EXERCISE

You'll need a profit and loss in CSV format for this exercise. Row 1 needs to be the names of the months. Column A needs to be the accounts. You can export a P&L from QuickBooks Desktop or get one from this book's resources ('PL 2024.csv'). Or you can copy the below-simplified text into a text file, then change the ending from ".txt" to ".csv".

,Jan,Feb
Total Income,34668,55775
Total COGS,20993.6,28953.23
Gross Profit,13674.4,26821.77
Total Expense,9856.42,8902.38
Net Income,3817.98,17919.39

Create a new document named "list_exercise.py". The first thing we're going to do is import packages. Now we haven't talked about packages yet because, up to this point, we've only used native python packages. Think of packages as spreadsheet add-ons or extensions. To use the add-on (package) in Python, you need to import it to the document you want to use it in.

```
import csv
import os
```

Note: Some packages must be installed from PyPI using pip before you can use them. Take your time with packages right now. We'll get to them in a later chapter. Right now, we will use packages installed by default with Python.

Now we will change the file directory that Python uses by adding the code below. Notice there is an "r" before the text. The "r" before the text lets you use backlashes in the text. It would help if you replaced the folder names with names from your computer folders.

```
os.chdir(r'C:\your_folder_name\folder_with_csv') #change folder names
```

Now we will import the data into python so we can use it:

```
with open('C:\your_folder_name\PL 2024.CSV', newline='') as f:
    reader = csv.reader(f)
    pl_2024 = list(reader)
print(pl_2024) #Numbers in this variable name referencing the year is ok
```

If you don't want to bother with the csv right now you can use this code to get pl_2024:

```
#Only use this if you are not importing the csv.
Pl_2024 = [['', 'Jan', 'Feb'], ['Total Income', '34668', '55775'], ['Total
COGS', '20993.6', '28953.23'], ['Gross Profit', '13674.4', '26821.77'],
['Total Expense', '9856.42', '8902.38'], ['Net Income', '3817.98',
'17919.39']]
```

From here, we want to add some variables to map out what's in the data. There are ways to do this more dynamically. We're just trying to keep things simple for now:

```
jan_column_index = 1
feb_column_index = 2

total_income_row_index = 1
cogs_row_index = 2
gross_profit_row_index = 3
total_expenses_row_index = 4
net_income_row_index = 5
```

Now the challenge is to use all of the above information to determine the following KPIs (don't worry about formatting at this point):

1. Gross Profit as a % of Income for both months
2. Total Expenses as a % of Income for both months
3. Net Income as a % of Income for both months
4. Dollar amount of sales increase for February over January
5. February Sales as a % of January Sales

Below are the answers in their respective order. I'll give you two hints:

1. Use backslash (\) to break the math equation into separate lines if they are too long. Division uses forward slash (/)
2. You'll need to change numbers that are string type to float type using the float() function.

Once you're ready, see the next page for the solutions:

```
gross_profit_percentage_jan = float(pl_report[total_income_row_index][jan_column_index]) \
                    /float(pl_report[gross_profit_row_index][jan_column_index])
gross_profit_percentage_feb = float(pl_report[total_income_row_index][feb_column_index]) \
                    /float(pl_report[gross_profit_row_index][feb_column_index])
print(f'Jan gross profit = {gross_profit_percentage_jan}')
print(f'Feb gross profit = {gross_profit_percentage_feb}')

expenses_as_percentage_jan = float(pl_report[total_income_row_index][jan_column_index]) \
                    /float(pl_report[total_expenses_row_index][jan_column_index])
expenses_as_percentage_feb = float(pl_report[total_income_row_index][feb_column_index]) \
                    /float(pl_report[total_expenses_row_index][feb_column_index])
print(f'Jan Expenses as % of Income = {expenses_as_percentage_jan}')
print(f'Feb Expenses as % of Income = {expenses_as_percentage_feb}')

net_income_as_percentage_jan = float(pl_report[total_income_row_index][jan_column_index]) \
                    /float(pl_report[net_income_row_index][jan_column_index])
net_income_as_percentage_feb = float(pl_report[total_income_row_index][feb_column_index]) \
                    /float(pl_report[net_income_row_index][feb_column_index])
print(f'Jan Net Income as % of Income = {net_income_as_percentage_jan}')
print(f'Feb Net Income as % of Income = {net_income_as_percentage_feb}')

month_over_month_sales_dollars_increase = \
                    float(pl_report[total_income_row_index][feb_column_index]) \
                    - float(pl_report[total_income_row_index][jan_column_index])
print(f'Feb Month Sales Dollar Increase = {month_over_month_sales_dollars_increase}')

month_over_month_sales_percentage_increase = \
                    float(pl_report[total_income_row_index][feb_column_index]) \
                    /float(pl_report[total_income_row_index][jan_column_index])
print(f'Feb Month Sales Percentage Increase = {month_over_month_sales_percentage_increase}')
```

TUPLES

Compared to lists, tuples are simpler. Since tuples cannot be added to, subtracted from, or changed in order, they are more straightforward. They come in handy when you want the code to stay consistent with sizes and values. Tuples can be used in lists as one widespread use. The distinction in syntax between lists and tuples is that you enclose tuples in parentheses () rather than square brackets []. Think of each tuple as a row in a spreadsheet to visualize the idea of tuples inside lists. Here are a few instances of using tuples in practice:

```
my_tuple = (1, 2, 'Bark', 4, 5, 5, 5)
print(my_tuple[2:])
print(len(my_tuple))
my_list_of_tuples = [('a','b','c'), ('e', 'f', 'g')]
print(my_list_of_tuples[0][0]) #print the first item in the first tuple
```

 Note: Tuples are faster than lists.

In Python, creating a tuple with one element is a bit tricky. Having one element within parentheses is not enough. We will need a trailing comma to indicate that it is a tuple. For example:

```
var1 = ("Hello") # string
var2 = ("Hello",) # tuple
```

SETS

To create a set you use curly brackets {} and add items inside like a list. Some examples:

```
my_set = {}
print(my_set)

another_set = {2, 3, 4}
print(another_set)
```

Although Sets look like tuples and lists there are major differences. One difference is you cannot have duplicate items in sets. For example:

```
my_list = [1, 2, 2, 2]
set_from_list = set(my_list) #Turn a List into a Set using set()
print(set_from_list) #Prints the unique values inside the list {1, 2}
```

 Note: A set can have any number of items and they may be of different types (integer, float, tuple, string etc.). But a set cannot have mutable elements like lists, sets or dictionaries as its elements.

I don't use sets very often, but there are some benefits. For example, it's faster to see if an item is inside a set than inside a list. Example:

```
print(1 in my_list) #A simple True, False question by using "in"
print(1 in set_from_list) #This search in a Set is faster then a list
```

Another key difference between Lists and Sets is we can't slice Sets or add Sets together like we can Lists. To add items to Sets, you need to use the add function of the Set. For example:

```
my_set = {}
myset.add('a')
print(my_set)
```

Python sets are:

- Unordered — The items of a set don't have any defined order
- Unindexed — We can't access the items with [i] as with lists
- Mutable — A set can be modified to integers or tuples
- Iterable — We can loop over the items of a set

Note: For a long time, sets didn't have an order in Python. Recent Python updates changed that, but I would still suggest thinking of them as having no order until you're further along in your Python education. For example, I still consider them as not having an order.

DICTIONARIES

Dictionaries in Python are based on key-value pairs. This means that each item in a dictionary has a key (something to look for) and a value (something to be returned). To create a dictionary, you use curly brackets {} similar to how you would create a set. Just like a set, each key in a dictionary must be unique. To access a value from a dictionary, you use the following syntax: dict_name[key_name]. This will return the value associated with that key. Now, let's dive into some examples:

```
my_dict = {'key_1':'value_1', 'key_2':'value_2'} #creating a dictionary
print(my_dict['key_2']) #prints 'value_2'
```

To add to a dictionary you add a value to a new key name. The syntax is like this: *dict_name[key_name] = value_a*. The value itself can be any object. Our example so far was a string. However, it can be an integer, list, another dictionary, tuple, set, etc. For example:

```
my_dict['key_3'] = [1, 2, 3]
print(my_dict) #{'key_1': 1, 'key_2': 'value_2', 'key_3': [1, 2, 3]}
print(my_dict['key_3'][1]) #Returns key_3 value, index 1 item
print(my_dict['key_1']) #Returns 'value_1'
my_dict['key_1'] = 1 #To re-assign the value of key_1 to the Integer 1
print(my_dict['key_1']) #Returns the Integer 1

print(my_dict.keys()) #Returns a list of the keys
print(my_dict.values()) #Returns a list of the values
print(my_dict.items()) #Returns a list of tuples like [(key, value)]
```

 Note: Here are some important points while using dictionary keys:

- You can't use the same key twice (no duplicate keys allowed).
- The values in the dictionary can be of any type, while the keys must be immutable like numbers, tuples, or strings.
- Dictionary keys are case sensitive (same key name but with the different cases are treated as different keys in Python dictionaries).

Dictionaries are extremely handy in all types of instances. Dictionaries in Python are a lot like JSON data in JavaScript. If you get a JSON object in Python, you'll most likely convert it to a Dictionary object before doing anything else.

CHAPTER 3 EXERCISE

Chapter 3's exercise is contained inside the supplemental material.

Functions And Statements

Congratulations you've reached chapter 4! From this point on, we'll start delving into more practical and useful applications. Up until now, you've been learning the fundamentals, akin to getting up on your hands and knees. From here, you'll begin to crawl!

MAIN STATEMENT

We'll start with the main statement, as it serves as the foundation for any useful script. The main statement is a specific line of code that initiates a script. Although it's relatively simple, it's essential to understand its basics. First, create a new folder named "Chapter4." Inside this folder, create a document named 'main_statement. py'. The document's name isn't crucial; it's just to ensure we're on the same page. Now, enter the following code and run it:

```
print(__name__) #two underscores 'name' two underscores
#Returns '__main__'
```

Notice that the returned response is "__main__". The code is requesting the document's name as referenced from within the document. The key point to remember is that the document from which you're running your script is always named "main". So, if you want to execute a program, what better way than to use a condition that will always evaluate to True? Consequently, the statement that officially starts your Python program should always be as follows:

```
def main():
    print('Whatever you want to do')

if __name__ == '__main__':
    main() #Initiates your main function
```

Now that you're familiar with the main statement, we'll return to it later to provide further explanation. First, however, you need to understand functions.

SPREADSHEET FUNCTIONS

Functions in Python are an excellent tool for organization. It's often impossible to accomplish everything within a single statement (typically one line). So, what should you do when you need multiple statements to achieve a particular goal? You create a function.

As spreadsheet experts, you're already familiar with the concept of functions and arguments, even if you might not realize it. Consider the cell where you input your text or formulas in your favorite spreadsheet program (refer to Figure 4.1).

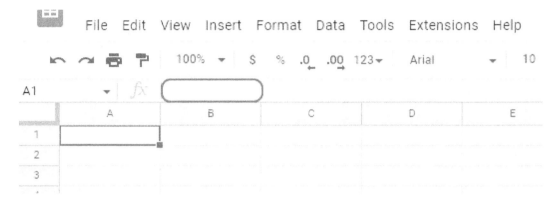

Figure 4.1

Notice the two letters "fx" beside the input box (on the left)? That's the mathematical shorthand for "function." And guess what – we're talking about essentially the same concept! A function in spreadsheet software is similar to a function in Python. If we break down a function in your spreadsheet software, we'll notice something interesting: spreadsheet functions also have arguments. Let's take the "IF" statement as an example. In a spreadsheet, you may have the following:

=if(A1=A2, "its true", "its false")

Let's break this down by replacing each part of the statement with the label of what each part is:

=function_name(argument_1, argument_2, argument_3)

The "IF" statement is a function with three arguments. The first argument (argument_1) must produce True or False. You can substitute the True or False value with a statement that could return True or False. The second argument (argument_2) is the value you want to be returned if argument_1 is True. The third argument (argument_3) is the value you want to be returned if argument_1 is False. Some time ago, programmers created this function and made it available for users like you. Now, you're going to learn how to create your own custom functions.

PYTHON FUNCTIONS

The syntax for a function in Python is as follows: You start with the keyword "def" (short for "definition"). By using "def", you're telling the computer that you're about to define a function name. After "def", you add the name you want for the function, which should be in snake_case (see Variables in Chapter 2) with all lowercase letters. After the name, you'll place parentheses () and include any "arguments" you want to use inside the function. Then, you'll have a colon ":" to end the definition statement of the function.

Remember how we discussed Code Blocks in Chapter 1? We're revisiting that concept now. After your definition statement, move to the next line and indent four spaces (you can also use the Tab key). This indentation tells Python that whatever you're about to write is within the scope of the function you just defined. Let's dive into some examples. Create a Python document named 'python_function_basics' and enter the following code:

```python
def three_plus_three():
    an_answer = 3 + 3
    return an_answer

#This function just prints an_answer it does not return anything.
def two_plus_something(a_number):
    an_answer = 2 + a_number
    print(an_answer)

#This function returns a variable named first_answer.
def do_some_math(argument_integer):
    #We call the function three_plus_three and assign the returned
    # value to the variable first_answer
    first_answer = three_plus_three()
    #we call the function two_plus_something but it doesn't return anything
    two_plus_something(argument_integer)
    return first_answer

if __name__ == '__main__':
    #We call the function do_some_math and pass the argument 5
    something_to_print = do_some_math(5)
    #notice do_some_math returns first_answer
    #but when returned we call it something_to_print
    print(something_to_print)
```

First, let's examine how Python reads and executes this code step by step:

1. Python starts reading the file from the top, proceeding line by line.
2. It encounters the function definition for three_plus_three and stores it in memory, making it available for future calls.
   a. Note that at this point the function is only available to be called. The function has not actually been called yet.
3. Moving further down, Python encounters the function definition for two_plus_something and stores it in memory as well.
4. Next, Python encounters the function definition for do_some_math and stores it in memory.

5. Python reaches the if __name__ == "__main__": statement and evaluates it.
6. Since the statement is True, Python enters the if block and calls the do_some_math function, passing the integer 5 as an argument.
    a. Inside the do_some_math function, the parameter "argument_integer" is assigned the value 5.
    b. Next the function "three_plus_three" is called.
        i. All of the lines in "three_plus_three" are executed.
        ii. In response, "three_plus_three" returns the integer 6. The variable "first_answer" is created and assigned the value of 6.
    c. Still inside "do_some_math", the function "two_plus_something" is called and passed the variable "argument_integer".
        i. All of the lines in "two_plus_something" are executed.
        ii. The last line prints the value of "an_answer" to the console
        iii. There is no return statement so Python returns None
    d. "do_some_math" returns the value of the variable "first_answer" (which is 6)
7. "something_to_print" is assigned the returned value from "do_some_math" (which is 6)
8. Python executes the statement "print(something_to_print)" and prints "6" to the console

By following these steps, we can gain a better understanding of how Python processes the code and the order in which functions are called and executed.

FUNCTION ARGUMENTS

We need to talk about the rules for arguments inside of functions. The best way to outline them is through a simple bullet point list:

- Do not set default values to required arguments.
    - Example: my_func(my_argument) vs. my_func(my_argument=1). my_argument=1 sets a default value to my_argument.
- Set default values to unrequired arguments.
    - Example: my_func(my_argument=1). my_argument=1 sets a default value to my_argument.
- If the quantity of non-keyword arguments is unknown use *args (arguments).
    - Examples: my_func(*args)
- If the quantity of keyword arguments is unknown use **kwargs (keyword arguments).
    - Examples: my_func(**kwargs)
- Order of arguments is important. It should go in the following order: Required, Not Required, args, kwargs.
    - Examples: my_func(required, not_required=1, *args, **kwargs)

Let's get some examples of the first two rules of when arguments are required. In the following code, I'll give correct and incorrect examples. Let's add the code to "function_arguments.py".

```
# This function has a required argument where the function will not run
# without it.
def my_func(required_arg):
    print(required_arg)

# This function adds the non-required argument.
# You make the argument not required by assigning a default value to it.
def my_func_not_required(required_arg, not_required_arg=None):
    print(required_arg)
    if not_required_arg:
        print(not_required_arg)
    else:
        print('No argument was passed to the optional argument')

# WRONG. You can't have a non-required argument before a required one.
def my_func_not_required(not_required_arg=None, required_arg):
    print(required_arg)
```

 Note: I don't use *args and **kwargs very often (if at all). I'm not saying they are useless; I usually substitute them for other things. Typically, I use a list if I have an indefinite length of things I need to pass as an argument. If I need a keyword value pair, I pass a dictionary. I include them in this book because you at least need to know about them. But I'm not going to use them in exercises. Here are some examples of their uses (also added to "function_arguments.py":

```
def sum_function(*args):
    total = 0
    for arg in args:
        total += arg
    return total

def sum_vegitables(*kwargs):
    vegetables = ['peas', 'carrots', 'corn']
    total = 0
    for key, value in kwargs.items():
        if key.lower() in vegetables:
            total += value
        print(key, ':', value)
    return total
```

 Note: The word "args" and "kwargs" are not required. What's required are the asterisks. One asterisk for single value, two asterisks for keyword value pair. You can substitute "*args" for "*numbers" or any other word (same with kwargs). That said, it's fairly standard to stick with args and kwargs as the words of choice.

FUNCTION EXERCISE

For this exercise you'll want to create a document named "functions_exercise.py". Inside the document add the following code:

```
def calculate_gross_margin():
    pass #pass is a place holder.  It just means ignore.

def calculate_net_income():
    pass

def main():
    sales = 100000
    cogs = 40000
    payroll = 10000
    marketing = 5000
    admin_expenses = 3000

    # Task 1: Add logic to calculate_gross_margin()
    # Task 2: Create the gross_margin variable and
    #         populate it from calculate_gross_margin
    # Task 3: Add logic to calculate_net_income using gross_margin
    # Task 4: Create the net_income variable and
    #         populate it form calculate_net_income

if __name__ == '__main__':
    main()
```

Give the problem a try on your own then go to the next page to look at a solution. There are a number of ways to tackle this problem so don't feel bad if your solution is different from mine.

FUNCTION EXERCISE SOLUTION

See below for my solution. You could have accomplished this differently. The main thing to realize is that if the code works that's what counts.

```
def calculate_gross_margin(sales, cogs):
    gross_margin = sales - cogs
    return gross_margin

def calculate_net_income(gross_margin, payroll, marketing, admin_expenses):
    net_income = gross_margin – payroll – marketing – admin_expenses
    return net_income

def main():
    sales = 100000
    cogs = 40000
    payroll = 10000
    marketing = 5000
    admin_expenses = 3000

    gross_margin = calculate_gross_margin(sales, cogs)
    net_income = calculate_net_income(gross_margin, payroll, marketing,
admin_expenses)

    print(net_income)
```

```
if __name__ == '__main__':
    main()
```

Net income should be 42000.

If, For, While Statements

IF STATEMENTS

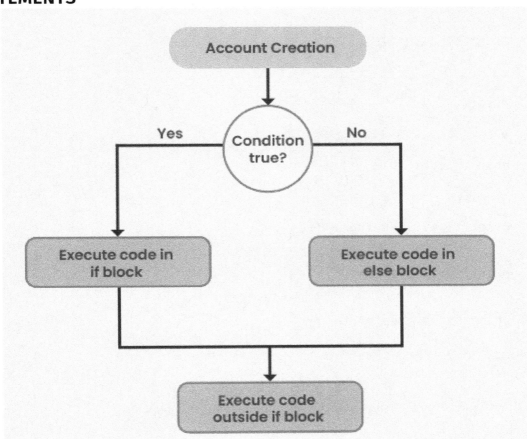

If statements in Python are quite straightforward, which contributes to the language's popularity. To practice, create a folder called "Chapter5". Inside the folder, create a file named "if_statements.py". You can find some examples below that you can add to the "if_statements.py" file.

```python
def main():
    # You would normally replace True below with some kind of comparison
    if True:
        # When the the if statement is true
        print('It is true!')

    # When false you can use an else statement to direct the flow
    if False:
        print('It is true!')
    else:
        print('it is false!')

    # elif adds another opportunity to compare
    if False:
        print('It is true!')
    elif False:
        print('It is true2!')
    else:
        print('it is false!')

    # Here is an example of actually comparing numbers
    if 2 == 1:
        print('It is true!')
    elif 2 >= 1:
        print('It is true2!')
    else:
        print('it is false!')

    x, y = 8, 8
    if (x < y):
        print("x is less than y")

    elif (x == y):
        print("x is same as y")

    else:
        print("x is greater than y")
if __name__ == '__main__':
    main()
```

Below are a few types of operators in Python you can use in your if statements:

Comparison Operators	Name	Example
==	Equal	if x == y:
!=	Not equal	if x != y:
>	Greater than	if x > y:
<	Less than	if x < y:
>=	Greater than or equal to	if x >= y:
<=	Less than or equal to	if x <= y:

Logical Operators	Name	Example
and	True if both statements are True	if x < 10 and x < 20:
or	True if either statement is True	if x < 10 or x > 20:
not	Reverses the result	if not(x < 10 or x > 20):

Identity Operators	Name (we'll cover objects in more detail in a later chapter)	Example
is	True if both are same object	if pl_statement is balance_sheet:
is not	True if both are not the same object	if pl_statement is not balance_sheet:

Membership Operators	Name	Example
in	True if a sequence is in another object (list, tuple, set)	a_list = [1, 2, 3] if 1 in a_list:
not in	True if both are not the same object	a_list = [1, 2, 3] if 5 not in a_list:

As you can imagine, there are many ways to use each operator. I'll use as many scattered through this course so you can see as many as possible in action. That is also an excellent time to google some ways to use each if it's still confusing.

FOR STATEMENTS:

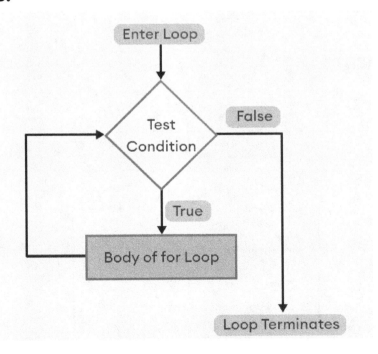

For loops are incredibly useful in Python. They provide an efficient way to iterate through various data structures, such as lists, dictionaries, and more. You'll find yourself using for loops so frequently that they'll become second nature. The syntax is quite similar to how you would write a sentence in English, which makes it easier to understand. The basic structure is as follows: "for variable_name in iterable_object:". Here are some examples to help you get started. You can save these in a file named for_statements.py."

```python
def main():
    list_a = [1, 2, 3, 4, 5, 6]
    for num in list_a:
        print(num)      #Prints each item in order

    years_to_compare = ['2020', '2021', '2022']
    for year in years_to_compare:
        print(year)

    #Notice you can unpack multiple elements especially in tuples
    multi_year_sales = [('2020', 50000), ('2021', 60000), ('2022', 70000)]
    for year, sales in multi_year_sales:
        print(f'Sales for {year} were {sales}!')

    #This is a good trick if you know how many times you want to loop
    for i in range(10):
        print(i)   #Notice i starts at zero

    #This is a good trick if you know how many times you want to loop
    for i in range(10):
        print(i)   #Notice i starts at zero

if __name__ == '__main__':
    main()
```

WHILE STATEMENTS

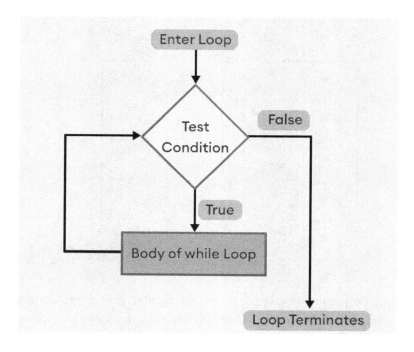

While loops can be risky if not used carefully. I recommend using them judiciously to avoid potential issues. It's not necessary to completely avoid them, but be aware that an improperly designed while loop can cause your computer to freeze. Due to this, we'll proceed with caution. I advise copying the provided code exactly as written until you gain more experience. If you accidentally freeze your computer, don't worry, it happens to everyone. Pressing Ctrl + Alt + Del can often help you regain control. If not, you may need to restart your computer using the power button.

The syntax for a Python while loop is as follows: "while condition_is_true: do_something()". To exit the loop, you can use the "break" statement or have the condition evaluate to False. Let's explore some examples that you can save in a file called "while_statements.py".

```python
def main():

    #Notice "finished" is printed after exiting the while loop:
    i = 0
    while i <= 10:
        print(i)
        i+=1 #This trick adds one number to the variable i
    print('finished')

    # Same thing except adding an else statement
    i = 0
    while i <= 10:
        print(i)
        i+=1 #This trick adds one number to the variable i
    else:
        print('I finished in the Else Statement')

    #This is the one that gets people in trouble if done incorrectly
    i = 0
    while True:
        #Sometimes programers don't add a break statement or an
        # iterator (i+=1) so a forever loop is born.
        # I'm adding i+=1 here so it won't keep going.
        if i < 10:
            print(i)
            i += 1
        elif i == 10:
            continue #continues to next iteration
            print('I will not ever print')
        else:
            print('I am at a break statement')
            break

if __name__ == '__main__':
    main()
```

Section 1 Exercises

PACKAGES

At this point, you're likely as eager as I am to dive into practical applications. We'll now explore some techniques that you can directly apply in your department and use at work. Keep in mind that there's still plenty to learn, so our options might be somewhat limited. Some concepts might be particularly challenging since we haven't covered objects yet (that's coming up in the next section). Don't feel discouraged if you don't grasp everything right away; we'll delve deeper into these topics as we progress through the material.

First, we need to install some packages that don't come bundled with Python by default. You can think of packages as add-ons for spreadsheet programs. In Python, we use a tool called Pip to manage package installations. I won't delve too deeply into the details of packages right now, as we'll cover them more extensively in a later chapter when we transition to PyCharm. Keep in mind that Thonny is a basic tool primarily used for learning, not production, so we won't be customizing it heavily. That being said, I want to provide you with something tangible as a reward for your dedication thus far.

To install packages in Thonny you go to Tools > Manage Packages. See figure 5.1.

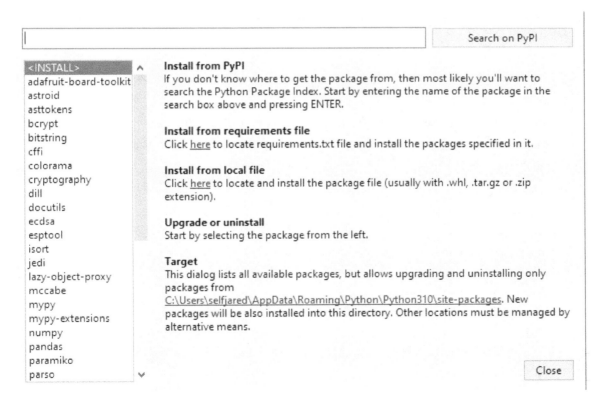

Figure 5.1

In the search field, you can enter the package name and then click on the "Search on PyPI" button. For our first package, we're going to search for "easygui." GUI stands for Graphical User Interface. Refer to Figure 5.2 for an example of what the search results should look like.

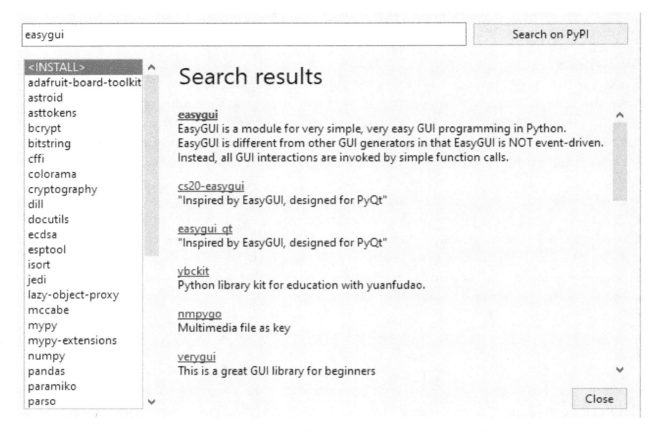

Figure 5.2

The first search result should be what we're looking for. After you click on the "easygui" in blue text you'll see more information on the package. You'll also see the "Install" button on the bottom. See figure 5.3. Click on the Install button and the package will install and be ready to use.

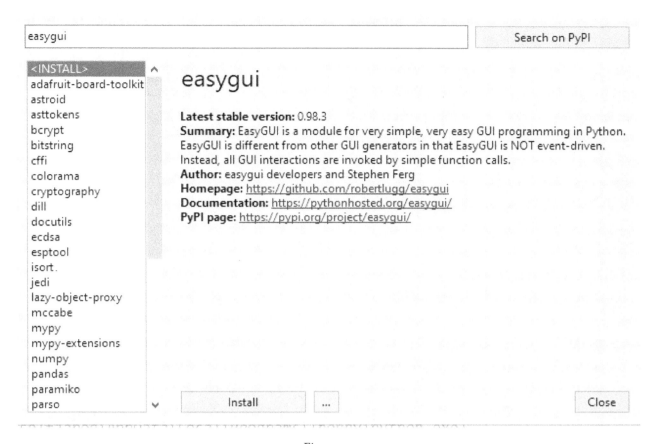

Figure 5.3

For this exercise we're going to install the following packages. Note that the packages need to be spelled exactly as I've spelled them below:

- easygui
- glob2
- pywin32

 Note: This exercise is designed around Microsoft Excel on a Windows operating system. If you're using a Mac there are many virtual programs you can use to run Windows and do this exercise.

COMBINING EXCEL REPORTS EXERCISE

In this exercise, we'll begin with financial reports in Excel. You can use any combination of reports in Excel or refer to this book's supplemental information. The reports used here were extracted from a QuickBooks desktop sample file. While it's possible to automate this process, for now, let's assume the reports were provided to us as-is. Our task is to combine and format them. You may notice some formatting issues with the reports, which could potentially be resolved by adjusting QuickBooks settings. However, for educational purposes, we'll keep the default QuickBooks formatting. We won't be focusing on formatting in this exercise, as that will be covered in a future chapter about working with Excel. It's important to consider alternative solutions, such as modifying settings, before developing a Python script to address an issue.

We'll name the file we're creating "exercise_combine_excel_reports.py." Start by including the necessary import statements and the main statement. Often, it's unclear which modules need to be imported until you begin coding, so don't worry about having a perfect import section at the outset. Your initial code should look like this:

```python
import os
import glob
import easygui
from win32com import client


def main():
    pass

if __name__ == '__main__':
    main()
```

 Note: There is a recommended order for organizing your import section. A simple rule of thumb is to order it from the most native to Python to the least native. In this example, the "os" package comes pre-installed with Python, making it as native as it gets. If you delve deeper into web development with Django, you may import Django-specific modules next, as they would be native to your project's base code. Packages like "glob" (glob2), "easygui", and "win32com" (pywin32) are all installed from PyPI and should be placed after your project's base code. Later, as we start importing functions and classes we create, these custom imports should be listed last in the import section.

The first task is to obtain user input. At the beginning of the code execution, we don't know the location of the folder containing the reports, the desired location for the final report, or the preferred name for the final report. While we could hard-code these values, it wouldn't provide an opportunity to learn how to gather user input. Therefore, we'll create a function called "get_user_input." This function will store the results in a dictionary named "user_input" and return it.

```python
def get_user_input():
    # We'll put the results in a dictionary. We need to
    # create an empty dictionary so we can add to it later.
    user_input = {}

    # easygui is a convenient way to interact with a user.
    #  for diropenbox and enterbox the function returns what the
    #  user selects.
    user_input['source_folder_location'] = easygui.diropenbox(
        default='~/Documents',
        title='Choose Folder Where Source Workbooks Are'
    )
    user_input['destination_folder_location'] = easygui.diropenbox(
        default=user_input['source_folder_location'],
```

```
        title='Choose Folder Where Final Workbook Should Go'
    )
    user_input['destination_workbook_name'] = easygui.enterbox(
        title='Name Your New Workbook',
        msg="Please Enter your new Workbook's name",
        default='2023_12_financials.xlsx'
    )

    # Instead of trusting that the user will add the .xlsx
    #   at the end of their file name we're going to test
    #   if they didn't add it. If not we'll add it.
    if user_input['destination_workbook_name'][-5:] != '.xlsx':
        # backslash (\) breaks a statement into multiple lines
        user_input['destination_workbook_name'] = \
            user_input['destination_workbook_name'] + '.xlsx'
    else:
        # I've found issues in the past with if statements that
        #   don't have an else to close it.  Although it's not
        #   technically required, I like to add them.
        pass

    # Python stores file and folder destinations with two back
    #   slashes instead of one.  The first tell the program that
    #   the second one should be taken literally and isn't a break
    user_input['destination_workbook_location'] = \
        (user_input['destination_folder_location']
        + '\\'
        + user_input['destination_workbook_name']
                                                    )
    return user_input
```

We'll add the "get_user_input" function to the top of the page after the imports, but before the main function. We'll then call the "get_user_input" function from our main function. So main should now look like this:

```
def main():
    user_input = get_user_input()
```

Once we have the user's input, we know where to start and finish the code. Now, we need to gather more information about the specific reports we'll be combining. To do this, we'll use a handy package called glob (glob2). The glob package allows you to search for files within folders. While it has other features, this capability alone makes it worth using. In our case, we're looking for all Excel files within a folder. To accomplish this, we'll first use the user input "source_folder_location."

When we print the string for the folder, it might look something like this: "C:\User Folder\My Project Folder." To use glob and search for Excel files, we'll add "\.xlsx" to the end of the string, so the final string will resemble: "C:\User Folder\My Project Folder\.xlsx." In SQL, the * (asterisk) serves as a wildcard. By using the asterisk, you're telling the computer to "search for any characters of any length." Therefore, "*.xlsx" will return any file in the folder with ".xlsx" as the last characters. Convenient, right? Here's our function:

```python
def get_source_workbooks_locations(user_input):
    # the * character is a wild card search in glob
    source_report_locations = /
        glob.glob(user_input['source_folder_location'] + '\\*.xlsx')
    print('report_locations = ' + str(source_report_locations))

    # Just in case the destination and source are the same location
    if user_input['destination_workbook_location'] in /
                            source_report_locations:
        os.remove(user_input['destination_workbook_location'])
        source_report_locations.remove(
                user_input['destination_workbook_location']
                )
    else:
        pass

    return source_report_locations
```

Add the function "get_source_workbooks_locations" right after "get_user_input". The returned value will be a list of excel files in the selected folder. As a result, we'll want to edit the main function so we can add that value to a new variable called "source_workbooks_locations". Change main to look like this:

```python
def main():
    user_input = get_user_input()
    source_workbooks_locations = get_source_workbooks_locations(user_input)
```

At this stage, we should have collected all the necessary information to take action. We'll now create a function that does more than just gather information. While projects aren't always this straightforward, in our case, gathering information and then doing something with it seems like the appropriate way to organize the workflow.

There are several ways to work with Excel in Python. Personally, I prefer using Microsoft's Component Object Model (COM). I won't delve into the details of using Excel and Python together at this moment, as there are other foundational principles I want to teach first that will make working with COM much easier. Once you grasp those concepts, you'll be able to write code for Word, PowerPoint, Excel, or any other COM object with relative ease. Even if we don't cover Excel later (though we will), mastering the other principles I teach will enable you to learn Excel on your own.

I mention this because I'm going to provide the next sections without much explanation. For now, I want you to have something tangible that you can actually use. If you've followed the code up to this point, the function "get_source_workbooks_locations" should end around line 45. Here's the rest of the code:

```python
def copy_sheet_to_sheet(
        excel,
        source_workbook_location,
        destination_report_location
        ):
```

```python
    # Extract names from the file locations
    source_workbook_name = source_workbook_location.split('\\')[-1]
    destination_workbook_name = destination_report_location.split('\\')[-1]

    # Create worksheet in destination workbook
    sheet_name = source_workbook_name.replace('.xlsx', '')
    excel.Windows(destination_workbook_name).Activate()
    excel.Sheets.Add().Activate()
    excel.ActiveSheet.Name = sheet_name

    # Copy source worksheet
    excel.Workbooks.Open(source_workbook_location)
    excel.Windows(source_workbook_name).Activate()
    excel.Sheets('Sheet1').Activate()
    excel.Cells.Select()
    excel.Application.CutCopyMode = False #For a failsafe
    excel.Selection.Copy()

    # Paste in destination worksheet
    excel.Windows(destination_workbook_name).Activate()
    excel.Sheets(sheet_name).Activate()
    excel.ActiveSheet.Paste()

    # Teardown
    excel.Application.CutCopyMode = False
    excel.Windows(source_workbook_name).Close()

def combine_reports(user_input, source_workbooks_locations):
    # Dispatch excel
    excel = client.Dispatch('Excel.Application')
    excel.Visible = True

    # Add the workbook
    excel.Workbooks.Add().SaveAs(Filename=user_input[
        'destination_workbook_location'
        ])
    excel.Workbooks.Open(user_input['destination_workbook_location'])

    # Copy the Sheets
    for source_workbook_location in source_workbooks_locations:
        copy_sheet_to_sheet(
                excel,
                source_workbook_location,
                user_input['destination_workbook_location'])

    # Teardown
    excel.Workbooks(user_input['destination_workbook_name']).Save()
    excel.Workbooks(user_input['destination_workbook_name']).Close()
    excel.Application.Quit()

def main():
    user_input = get_user_input()
```

```
    source_workbooks_locations = get_source_workbooks_locations(user_input)
    combine_reports(user_input, source_workbooks_locations)


if __name__ == '__main__':
    main()
```

If you think to yourself, "This code looks a lot like VBA," you're absolutely right—I took it directly from VBA. If you're reading this book, there's a good chance you've used VBA once or twice in your career. If not, don't worry; it's not a prerequisite. However, if you have experience with VBA, you'll feel right at home incorporating all that VBA knowledge into your new Python programs.

SECTION 2

PROJECTS AND OBJECTS

Up until now, we've worked on simple single-document projects using Thonny. While this is suitable for beginners, as you gain more experience with the basics, you'll want to switch to a more advanced IDE (Integrated Development Environment). In this book, I'll teach you how to use the paid version of PyCharm. That being said, almost everything we cover will also be supported in PyCharm Community Edition (which is free). Another popular IDE is Visual Studio Code (also free). Unfortunately, this book cannot cater to every preference, so I will focus on teaching you using arguably the best IDE available for Python developers: PyCharm Professional. If you choose to use a different tool, you're welcome to do so, but you may need to rely on Google to figure out how to implement some of the concepts discussed in this book within your chosen IDE.

CHAPTER 6

PyCharm, Environments, Git

There are numerous videos available online that explain how to download and install PyCharm, so I won't cover that process here (you can easily find these tutorials on YouTube). Instead, I'll focus on what you need to know for the accounting tasks we plan to undertake and share insights on how I've learned to navigate PyCharm effectively. With that in mind, I'll assume that you've already installed PyCharm and are ready to proceed.

PYTHON

Up to this point, we've allowed Thonny to manage Python and environments for the sake of convenience. Now, we need to begin handling these aspects on our own. I won't delve too deeply into Python versions, but it's important to know that each new version introduces new features and modifies existing ones.

In the accounting world, you can't open a newer copy of a company file with an older version of the program. For instance, if you create a backup copy of a QuickBooks company file in Enterprise 22.0, you can't open it with Enterprise 21.0 (an earlier version). Similarly, in Excel, it's not recommended to open documents created with the latest version of Excel using Excel 2013. Compatibility issues also exist when moving in the opposite direction.

Python has major versions like Python 2 and Python 3. As of this writing, Python 3.11 has been released. You shouldn't run programs with an earlier version of Python than what they were created in. For example, don't run Python 3.6 on a program developed using Python 3.7. The other direction works, but just like in Excel or QuickBooks Desktop, the further removed you are from the original version, the greater the potential issues.

All the examples I've provided up to this point were created in Thonny using Python 3.10. Although 3.11 has been released, I recommend continuing this book with Python 3.10 to avoid compatibility issues.

To download and install earlier versions of Python for Windows, go to:

https://www.python.org/downloads/windows/

 Note: Later in the book, I'll teach you how to interact with QuickBooks Desktop directly. If you want to learn that section, you'll need to install the 32-bit version of Python. If you don't plan on learning that, you can install the 64-bit version.

You'll want to choose an option that says "Download Windows installer (XX-bit)" under Python 3.10.XX.

I'll leave it to the numerous YouTube videos available that walk you through installing Python. You'll also want to ensure Python is added to your system PATH (there are plenty of videos on this as well). When you've completed the installation, you should be able to open a command prompt in Windows, type in "python --version", and see "Python 3.10.XX" displayed (with X replaced by the minor version number).

 Note: While it is possible to have multiple versions of Python installed on the same machine, this can introduce additional complexity that you may not be prepared to handle. For now, I recommend choosing one version of Python and sticking with it until you feel comfortable creating projects, setting up virtual environments, and assigning interpreters. If you're not familiar with these concepts, it's a sign that you're not ready for managing multiple Python versions. If you already have multiple versions installed, ensure the PATH version for Python is set to the main version you want to use. You don't necessarily need to uninstall any other versions.

PROJECTS

In PyCharm, projects can be compared to new company files in QuickBooks Desktop. Each company file has its unique settings, can only be opened in a specific version, contains its own chart of accounts, and maintains its own data.

Similarly, PyCharm projects have their own settings, should only be run in the version of Python they were created in, and can have different configurations. Generally, you would create a new project for each application you intend to develop. For instance, if you need to create custom sales integrations for Bob's online store, you would start a new project. If you want to design a program that collects banking transactions for all your clients, you would create another separate project.

ENVIRONMENTS

Environments can be thought of as project settings. Although it's not an exact comparison, it serves as a helpful analogy. Environments begin with a specific version of Python you have installed. For the rest of this book, when you create a project in PyCharm, you'll choose "Pure Python" in the left column. You'll create a new environment using "Virtualenv" and choose the Base interpreter as Python 3.10. See figure 6.1 for a look at what the settings typically look like for each project I create.

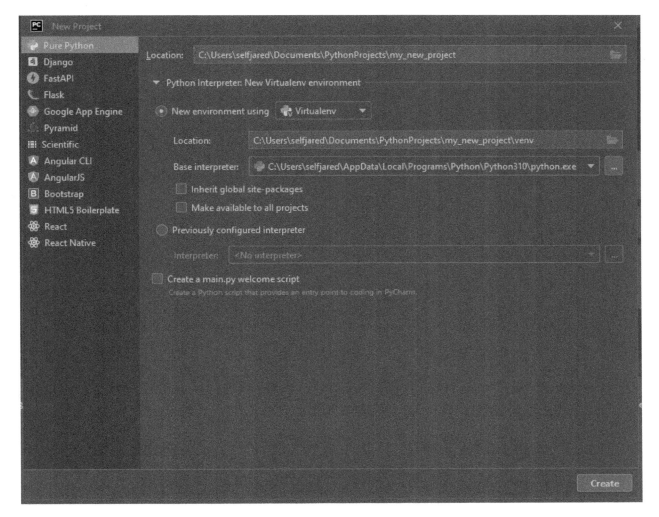

Figure 6.1

I'm not going to go into the details of Virtual Environments at this stage. For now, just think of environments as if you're choosing which version of QuickBooks Desktop you want to use as the default when opening a QuickBooks Company File. Just like that, we're selecting the default environment we'll use when opening our project in PyCharm.

To create a project and virtual environment for all the work you did in Section 1, follow these steps:

1. Open PyCharm.
2. If it opens to the "Welcome to PyCharm" window, choose the "New Project" button. If it opens to your last project, go to File > New Project.
3. In the "Location" box, choose the parent folder to all the Chapter Folders you created earlier. In this example, select the folder named "AccountingPy" which contains each Chapter Folder as subfolders.

By following these steps, you'll create a new PyCharm project and virtual environment with Python 3.10 as the base interpreter. This will provide a consistent and organized structure for your Python projects related to accounting. See figure 6.2.

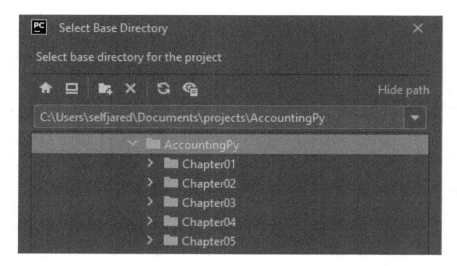

Figure 6.2

Once you select the parent folder, you'll click on the "OK" button. You'll get a warning that the "Directory Is Not Empty". Click on the button "Create from Existing Sources". See figure 6.3.

Figure 6.3

If you created the project as I described, you'd see "Python 3.10" on the bottom right of PyCharm. See figure 6.4.

Figure 6.4

If you haven't followed my instructions you may see something like "<No interpreter>". See figure 6.5.

Figure 6.5

In PyCharm, if anything says "interpreter" what it's referring to is the virtual environment. It's PyCharm's way of asking what environment should be used to run the code in the project. Regardless of if it says No interpreter or a version of Python, click on it now. You should get a list of interpreters and the options to go to interpreter settings or "Add Interpreter". Click on "Add Interpreter". The first option in the left column should be "Virtualenv Environment". When Virtualenv Environment is selected you'll see the "Add Python Interpreter" window and you'll be prompted to either create a new environment or add an existing environment. See figure 6.6.

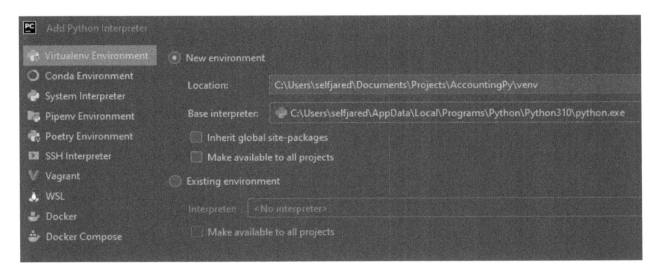

Figure 6.6

Right now, we won't create a new environment. I'm showing you this mainly to help you decide which interpreter to use. Pycharm's other components come together organically once you've selected your interpreter. For instance, the "Add Configuration..." button is located in the top right corner. See figure 6.7.

Figure 6.7

Instead of using the "Add Configuration" button in PyCharm, you can automatically configure your project settings by running your Python script. Here's how you can do that:

1. Open the Python script file you want to run within your project. Make sure it's the main script or the entry point of your project (e.g., main.py).

2. Right-click anywhere within the script's text editor area.
3. From the context menu, click on "Run 'your_script_name'" (e.g., "Run 'main'"). This action will create a new run configuration for your script automatically.

By doing this, PyCharm will automatically create a run configuration for your project, which includes settings like the Python interpreter (virtual environment) and the script to be executed. This method is more straightforward and easier to manage compared to manually adding configurations.

In the future, you can simply click on the green "play" button in the top-right corner of the PyCharm window or press Shift+F10 to run the same script with the same configuration. You can also access the list of available run configurations using the drop-down menu next to the "play" button.

RUNNING YOUR PROGRAM

I've explained in "Environments" how to add an interpreter to PyCharm. I'm starting with the assumption that you have an interpreter selected. If not, go back to that section and add the interpreter. You may need to create a virtual environment if you haven't already.

If you're running the program for the first time, I find it simplest to right click on the Python file and select "Run". Go ahead and run Chapter01>hello_world.py. See figure 6.8.

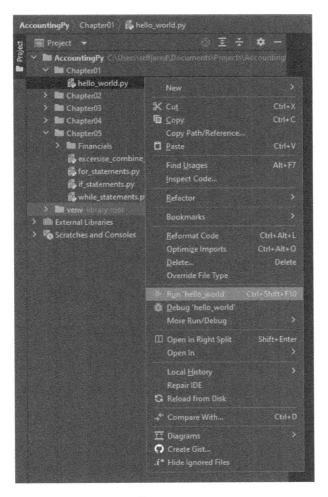

Figure 6.8

You'll notice after running hello_world.py that the top right corner is now configured. See Figure 6.9.

Figure 6.9

Also, notice the terminal at the bottom where the text "Hello World!" was printed. See figure 6.10.

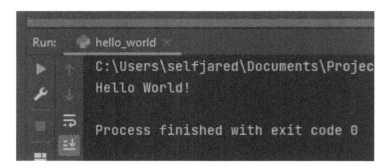

Figure 6.10

PIP AND PYPI

Try to run the program in Chapter05>excersise_combine_excel_reports.py. You should get the error "ModuleNotFoundError". When we ran the program in Thonny, we installed the packages we needed inside the environment Thonny created. Now we're in a new environment and need to add the packages to this environment. On the bottom of PyCharm you should have a number of tabs available like "Version Control", "Run", "Python Packages", etc.. We could use the "Python Packages" tab and install the packages there. Instead, we're going to use the command line inside the "Terminal" tab.

Click on the tab that says "Terminal". When you open a terminal in PyCharm the virtual environment (venv) is activated for you. See figure 6.11. This helps you know that you're in the correct environment for your project. Type in and run the following commands one at a time:

- pip install easygui
- pip install glob2
- pip install pywin32

You can use the packages created by the Python community on PyPI. The command used to access the PyPI repository is called pip. When you install packages using the Python Packages tab, PyCharm starts a command line in the background and executes the "pip install..." command for you. Most of the time, typing it in yourself is just quicker.

GIT AND VERSION CONTROL

Git is a powerful tool on its own, and version control is certainly an aspect that we, as accountants, should embrace. However, I won't delve too deeply into the specifics of using Git. For the most part, accountants will likely utilize Git in the same manner as other programmers. To learn Git, I recommend looking into gamified learning approaches. By searching "Git gamification" on Google, you'll find numerous helpful resources.

With that being said, I'll share my personal approach to using Git. First, I created a GitHub account. Whenever I start a new project, the initial step I take is to add a .gitignore file to the project and commit it to my GitHub repository. The .gitignore file contains various entries, but it's primarily a file that I copy and paste from one project to another. I'll include a copy of the .gitignore file I use in this book's resources.

From that point on, I manage Git using the VCS dropdown in PyCharm. I maintain a "main" branch and a "dev" branch. The main branch contains a stable version of my program, while the dev branch serves as a pre-production environment. Whenever I want to introduce new functionality to my program, I create branches from the dev branch. I make it a habit to commit frequently as I work. Once I'm satisfied with the added functionality, I merge my branch back into the dev branch. In such a scenario, if another programmer were collaborating with me, they could also branch off from the dev branch. After ensuring that everything in the dev branch works as expected, I push the changes to the main branch and use the main branch for production purposes.

If all that seemed confusing, don't worry about it for now. To start, it's perfectly fine to have a single main branch and no other branches. Focus on adding commits and pushing those commits to GitHub daily. By doing so, you'll minimize the risk of permanently losing your work. Also, ensure that you set your projects to private until you're ready to make them public.

 Note: Remember that the Commit Message is important, and people will judge you based on it. Keep it simple by stating what you've accomplished with the commit. Avoid writing anything inappropriate, leaving the message blank, or being dismissive, as others will evaluate your work based on these messages.

PROJECT ORGANIZATION

Python has some interesting ways it structures its projects and there are a lot of opinions on this topic. I'm less concerned about outlining the exact way your file structure should be handled and more concerned you understand why some file are where they are. These files are typically on the top level of the project:

- The .gitignore file provides a list of items you don't want to push to GitHub.
- Main.py (where your code will be executed from)
- Venv, which PyCharm created. (You won't create this folder by hand.)

When you create a folder within a Python project, it's often a good idea to create a "Python Package." This helps organize your code into modular units, making it easier to maintain and understand. To create a Python Package in PyCharm:

1. Make sure you have your project file tree open on the left side of the PyCharm window.
2. Right-click on the parent folder (in your case, it's called "AccountingPy") to bring up a dropdown menu.
3. Hover over "New" in the dropdown menu, and then click on "Python Package." See figure 6.11.

By doing this, you'll create a new folder with an empty __init__.py file inside. This file tells Python that the folder is a package and can be imported as a module in your code.

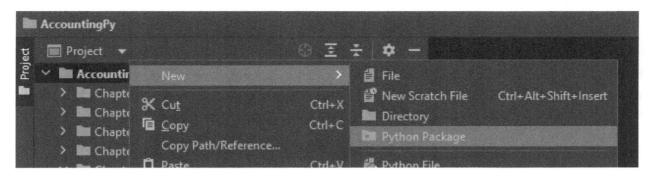

Figure 6.11

By creating a folder with the __init__.py file, you're telling Python to treat the folder as a package and search for Python files within it. A directory without the __init__.py file, such as a folder containing only static resources like images, wouldn't be treated as a Python package and wouldn't be searched for code.

By reaching this point in your learning journey, you should feel more comfortable using PyCharm or any other IDE you've chosen. The reason we waited until now to dive into this topic is that it's essential for you to have a basic understanding of Python and the ability to perform some tasks without being overwhelmed by environment management and other complexities.

Now that you have a solid foundation and some experience, you're prepared to tackle more advanced topics and take your Python skills to the next level. Keep up the good work, and remember that practice and persistence are key to mastering any new skill!

REFACTOR INSTEAD OF RENAME, MOVE, OR DELETE

It's important to highlight the usefulness of modern IDEs when it comes to refactoring code. When you want to rename or delete something, look for the term "Refactor" in your IDE. For example, in PyCharm, right-click on a name and choose "Refactor" to access options like "Rename." PyCharm will not only rename the function or variable in the current location but also update all references to that name throughout the code. This can save you a significant amount of time and effort compared to manually searching for and updating each reference.

Refactoring also allows you to move classes and functions to different locations within your project structure. This is another useful feature that can help streamline your code organization and maintenance. See figure 6.12 for an example of how to access refactoring options in PyCharm.

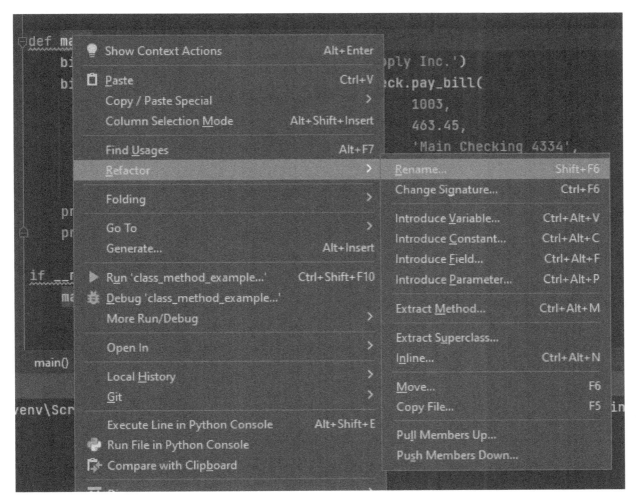

Figure 6.12

EXERCISE

For this exercise, we will explore how to access other modules in a basic app structure. To prepare for this exercise, you need to complete the following steps:

1. Install the package "python-decouple" from PyPI using the command: pip install python-decouple.
2. Create a folder named "Chapter6".
3. Inside the "Chapter6" folder, create the following folders and maintain the hierarchy as shown in figure 6.12 and below.

This is the hierarchy you should have:

- main.py
- settings.py
- .env
- .gitignore

- my_app (a "Python Package")
  - __init__.py
  - file_with_extra_functionality.py

Figure 6.12

Inside .gitignore add the below code.

```
venv
.idea
.env
```

Inside "file_with_extra_functionality.py" add the following code:

```python
import easygui

def select_something():
    selections = None
    while selections is None:
        easygui.msgbox("I'm going to loop until you decide!")
        selections = easygui.multchoicebox(
            title='Pick Something',
            msg="If you don't pick I'll just keep looping",
            choices=[
                'Profit and Loss',
                'Balance Sheet',
                'AP Report',
                'AR Report'
            ]
        )
    else:
        selection_yn = easygui.ynbox(title="You Decided!!!",
            msg="It's about time you decided!\n" \
            "Want to see what you selected?")
        if selection_yn:
            easygui.msgbox(title='Your Selections', msg=selections)
        else:
            easygui.msgbox(title='Goodbye', msg='Have a nice day!')
```

Inside ".env" file add the following code:

```
USERNAME=AccountingPy
PASSWORD=AccountingPyRocks!
```

Inside settings.py add the following code:

```
from decouple import config

USERNAME = config('USERNAME')
PASSWORD = config('PASSWORD')
```

And finally inside main.py add this code:

```
from my_app.file_with_extra_functionality import select_something
from settings import *

def main():
    some_extra_thing_i_want_done()
    print(USERNAME)
    print(PASSWORD)

if __name__ == '__main__':
    main()
```

Inside main.py we are importing the function "select_something" from the "file_with_extra_functionality. py" file inside of the "my_app" folder. We then imported all of the variables from settings using the wildcard asterisk (*).

I've also introduced another new feature with ".env". The basic idea is you don't want to add sensitive data to github (like usernames and passwords). If you do, you could accidentally share that information with the world. So you create a "settings.py" file that can get environment data from your local environment (".env"). In settings.py you can create the necessary variables needed at runtime then use them as needed. In this case we're just printing them out to the console.

DEBUGGER

Pycharm's Debugger is Pycharm's secret weapon. I use it often to actually write my code. Let me explain. When you're trying to build a program to do something you're not always going to be able to memorize the values of every variable you created. Especially when you import data into your program you could get all kinds of things you don't expect. Pycharm's debugger allows you to pause the program mid run and look at the different objects as they actually are. Then you can manipulate and play with those objects to figure out what works and what doesn't. Once you figure out what works you simply add it to your code.

Let's take the exercise we just did into consideration. Open the file Chapter6>my_app>file_with_extra_functionality.py in pycharm. On the left bar between the code and the line numbers click to add a red dot on the "while selections is None:" line of the code. In my case it's line 5. See the red dot on the left of figure 6.13.

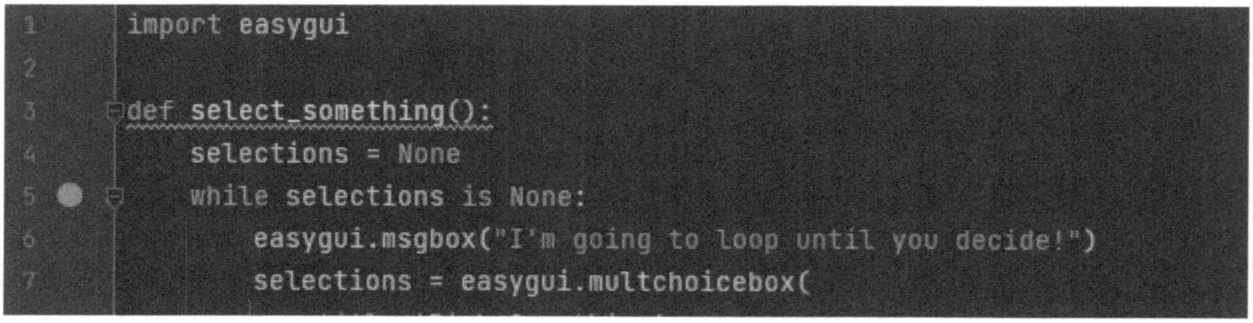

```
1    import easygui
2
3    def select_something():
4        selections = None
5  ●      while selections is None:
6            easygui.msgbox("I'm going to loop until you decide!")
7            selections = easygui.multchoicebox(
```

Figure 6.13

Now instead of running the code we're going to run the debugger. To run the debugger you can right click on the tab in pycharm and underneath "Run" you'll see the option "Debug". Or you can hit the debug icon on the top right. Or in the menu bar click on Run>Debug. The main thing you're looking for is the debug icon. See figure 6.14.

Figure 6.14

Now remember we enter this code from the main.py file so you need to start the debugger from that file. Once you start the debugger you'll notice it stops the program at the line with the red dot. See figure 6.15.

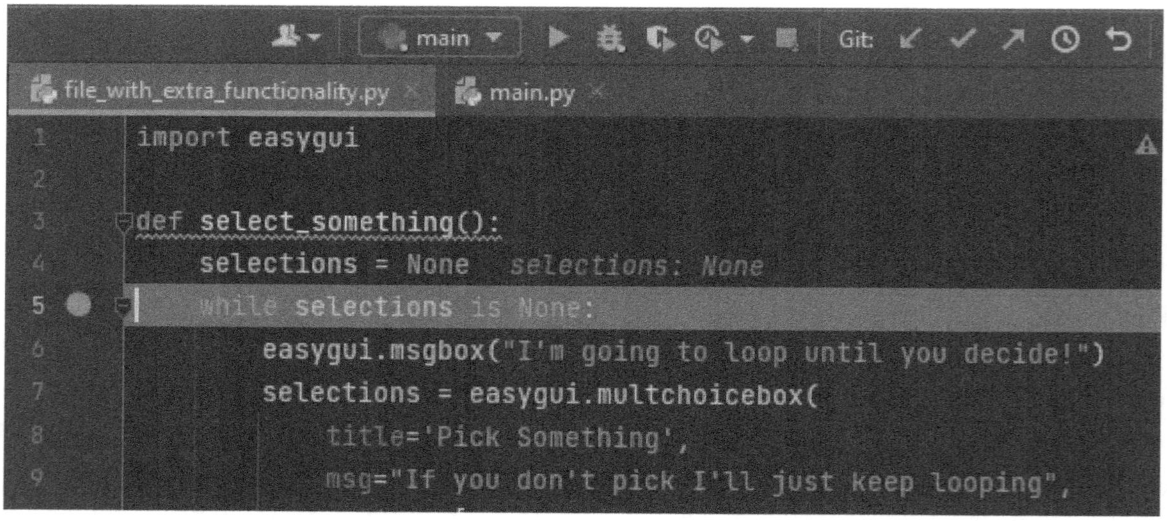

```
     file_with_extra_functionality.py ×      main.py ×
1        import easygui
2
3        def select_something():
4            selections = None    selections: None
5  ●          while selections is None:
6                easygui.msgbox("I'm going to loop until you decide!")
7                selections = easygui.multchoicebox(
8                    title='Pick Something',
9                    msg="If you don't pick I'll just keep looping",
```

Figure 6.15

Also notice on the bottom the Debug window is now up. See figure 6.16.

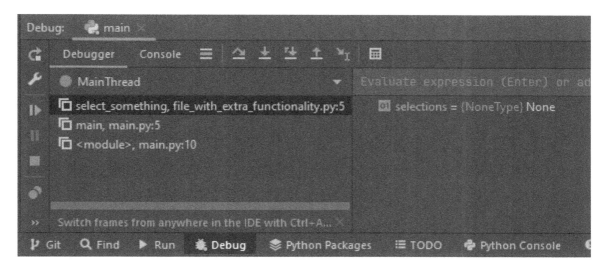

Figure 6.16

The bottom debug window is where all the fun happens. First, notice there are two tabs on the top, one titled "Debugger" with a blue line under it and the other titled "Console". Right now you're in the Debugger tab. In the Debugger tab, you have the exact hierarchy of where you are in the code. In this example there are 3 layers. According to figure 6.16, the bottom is main.py line 10. The next up is the main function in main.py line 5. Next up is the select_something function in the file_with_extra_functionality.py file line 5.

You can click on each of those different lines and see on the right window how the variables change according to the scope of the line you selected. For example if you click on the bottom line you'll see you have access to the "PASSWORD" and "USERNAME" variable. See figure 6.17.

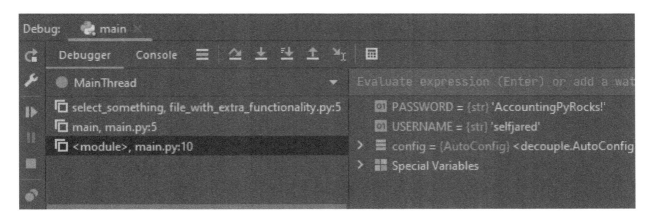

Figure 6.17

What's handy at this point is the variables on the right. If you click on the arrow next to "config" in the right window you'll get a dropdown of the attributes that are inside the config variable at the exact moment the code is paused. See figure 6.18.

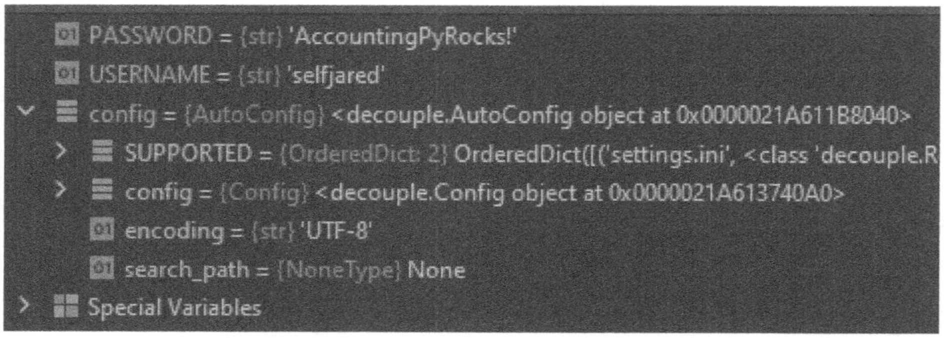

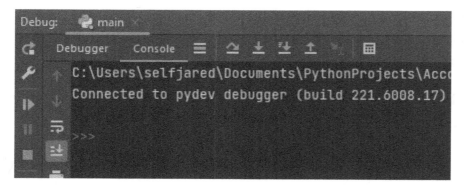

Figure 6.18

Hopefully you can begin to see how incredibly handy this is. I don't know about you but I can't always memorize everything a computer can hold in memory at any given moment. Well this solves that problem by giving you exactly what's in memory at any given point.

If you then click on the Console tab you would see a console line as if you were in main.py line 10 in the middle of the code running. See figure 6.19.

Figure 6.19

In that python console you can write code and play with the environment. Try changing the "USERNAME" variable by typing "USERNAME = 'new_user'" inside the console (then hit enter). If you go back to the Debugger tab you'll notice you changed the "USERNAME" variable's value in the right hand tab. You just made a manual change in the middle of run-time. Notice in the left window if you click on other lines the variable on the right changes. This represents the scope changes as you go through the code.

While programming, I prefer to pause my program at a point where I plan to add new lines of code. I then try out my intended code in the console to see if it produces any errors or achieves the desired outcome. If it works as expected, I incorporate the tested lines into the actual code. This approach allows me to test my code while creating it. I encourage you to experiment with this feature and find ways to integrate it into your development workflow.

CHAPTER 7

Objects

 Note: Sometimes I'll use the term "Object" instead of Class or Instance. When I do, I mean it to reference both Class and Instance. If I use the term "Class" or the term "Instance" I mean what I say..

Until now, we've primarily been experimenting with Python. Objects, however, are where things truly get serious. When I first started learning Python, I encountered numerous tutorials about objects, often using analogies like planes, trains, and automobiles. I suggest you explore at least one of these explanations to better relate to other programmers. If you don't, it might be like discussing the first Avengers movie without having watched the original Iron Man film – you'll simply be missing crucial context.

Learning about Object Oriented Programming (OOP) principles through traditional methods never really helped me understand how to apply it to my accounting work. I found it challenging to decide when to create an object versus a function or something else. Consequently, for a while, I used Python to create large, complex functions for everything, essentially ignoring everything beyond the basic structure of objects in Python. This significantly limited my ability to comprehend the code I was working with. I would attempt to reverse engineer something I found and apply it to accounting, but struggled to understand the original code.

As I gained more knowledge about objects in Python, I gradually discovered ways to apply them to my code in a manner that made sense for accounting. My goal is to spare you the headaches I experienced by sharing what I've learned. Hopefully, this will enable you to understand and utilize objects much earlier than I did.

ABSTRACTION

Abstraction is a fundamental principle in programming and should feel pretty familiar to accountants. We use abstraction all the time, we just don't use the word. Let's take the Balance Sheet for an example of abstraction. A Balance Sheet is an abstraction of many smaller parts. For example: It's the sum of all transactions in the checking account, it has liabilities which are an abstraction of company debt, you perform reconciliations which is an abstraction of the procedure of checking your books against external statements. The three main abstraction forms in programing are the following:

1. Data abstraction: Creating abstract data types that hold data and operations you can perform on that data. For example, a bill payment is a check that was written and sent to a vendor to pay down a balance. We use abstraction to call it a bill payment instead of all of the things bill payment represents.

2. Procedural abstraction: This involves breaking down a complex task into smaller, more manageable procedures or functions. For example, a reconciliation is an abstraction of a bunch of smaller tasks like collecting statements, selecting an account, selecting a transaction, etc..

3. Object-oriented abstraction: This involves creating classes that encapsulate data and behavior, allowing developers to create complex systems using simple, reusable components. For example, a payroll check could be a class. It could have data like SUTA and FUTA tax. Then a procedure like calculating FUTA tax. Saying "calculate_futa" in your code is a lot easier than writing every step, every time it's calculated.

In summary, abstraction is a powerful concept in programming that allows developers to simplify complex systems or concepts, making them easier to understand, modify, and reuse. You don't need to memorize this word or the three types, I'm just bringing the word to your awareness.

OBJECT BASICS

At their core, objects should represent real-life entities. In regular programming, these can be cars, rabbits, or planes. In accounting, they might be invoices, accounts, vendors, etc. Objects have attributes (qualities or characteristics of the object) and methods (actions the object can perform, i.e., verbs). Take a look at the following code that creates an Invoice class. You can add this code to a new folder named "Chapter07" in a file called "object_basics.py":

```python
class Invoice():

    def __init__(self, doc_number):
        self.doc_number = doc_number

    def change_doc_number(self, new_doc_number):
        self.doc_number = new_doc_number

def main():
    invoice = Invoice(1001) # Actually Creates The Object
    print(invoice.doc_number) # Prints the doc_number attribute's value
    invoice.change_doc_number(1002)
    print(invoice.doc_number) # Will Print 1002

if __name__ == '__main__':
    main()
```

 Note: When naming classes, you should use the CapWords convention. This means the first letter of every word is capitalized, and there are no underscores.

To create an "Instance" from a "Class", you call the class like you would a function. Then, you pass in the arguments after the first one (with the first argument being "self" and reserved for referencing the class within itself). In this case, we created the variable "invoice", which is an instance of the "Invoice" class. Notice that the variable is in camel_case. Up until now, the values of variables have been instances of the Integer Class, List Class, String Class, etc.

It's essential to understand the distinction between Classes and Instances. Classes are not Instances; they are templates for instances. In accounting software, you may look at an invoice template and even print it out. However, until it has a reference number, amount due, etc., it's just a template. It becomes an instance when you actually do something with it.

To access an attribute or method in a Python object, type the name of the object (instance or class), followed by a period, and then the name of the attribute or method. In this example, it's "invoice.doc_number" to access the "doc_number" attribute of the "invoice" variable (an instance of the Invoice Class). We would use "invoice.change_doc_number(1002)" to utilize the "change_doc_number" method of the Invoice object. We always ignore the first argument ("self") of a method in a class and start with the second argument.

__INIT__ METHOD

Let's examine the first method inside the class, the "init" method. When we create an instance of a class, everything inside the init method is executed. The init method is known as a constructor, meaning it's run upon creation. Notice that the first argument for the init method is "self". This is not a play on my last name; it's a standard in Python. The variable "self" is used inside a class to reference itself within the class's code. In this case, it assigns the value of the "doc_number" argument to the "doc_number" attribute (self.doc_number = doc_number).

The second argument of the init method is "doc_number". This is a regular argument, just like all the other function arguments we've seen so far in the book. This argument is passed into the init method when we create an instance of the Invoice class. In this case, the argument is required because it is not assigned a default value.

PRIVATE METHODS AND ATTRIBUTES

Another useful feature is the ability to create private and protected methods and attributes. When creating classes, you may not want all of the methods and attributes to be accessible from an instance. As a result, if you start the name of a method with a single underscore, you're telling Python you want that method to be private. This means you can use the code when programming inside the class, but you generally can't access it outside of the class. For example, when working on a method inside the class, you can use the private methods and attributes in your code without a problem. However, if you create an instance inside your main function and try to use the private attribute or method, you can't. In reality, there are workarounds to see and use the private attributes and methods, but we won't go into that in this book. See the code below, which I'll put in "private_methods_and_attributes.py":

```python
class MyClass:
    def __init__(self, value):
        self._value = value #This is a private value

    def get_value(self): # This gets the private value
        return self._value

    def set_value(self, value): # This sets the private value
        self._value = value
```

```python
    def _private_method(self):
        print("This is a private method")

    def public_method(self):
        print("Value:", self._value)
        self._private_method()

def main():
    obj = MyClass(42)
    obj.public_method()   # Output: "42"
    obj._private_method()   # AttributeError

if __name__ == '__main__':
    main()
```

PROTECTED METHODS AND ATTRIBUTES

Protected methods and attributes are similar to private methods and attributes, but they offer more security. Although there are ways to access and change private attributes and methods from an instance of a class (not covered in this book), you can't access protected methods or attributes from an instance. A protected attribute or method starts with two underscores instead of one underscore, like private ones. I tend not to create them very often, if ever. I'm not saying they aren't useful; I just want you to be aware of them for now.

TYPE CASTING

Type casting in Python refers to the process of converting a value from one data type to another data type. Python provides several built-in functions for type casting, including:

- int(): Used to convert a value to an integer data type.
- float(): Used to convert a value to a floating-point data type.
- str(): Used to convert a value to a string data type.
- bool(): Used to convert a value to a boolean data type

A strength and challenge with Python is that variables can be created and changed without having to declare them ahead of time. This is advantageous because it allows for greater flexibility when working through your code. However, it can also be problematic, as a variable might be of the wrong type when received as an argument. This is why type hinting was introduced. Type hinting enables the programmer to specify the expected types for arguments and the expected return type for methods. This makes the code more readable and easier to maintain. To use type hinting, you typically place a colon after the variable name, followed by the type. See the example below, which you can find in "type_hint_example.py".

```python
from datetime import date, datetime

class Contact:
    def __init__(self, name: str, email: str, phone: str, DOB: date):
        self.name: str = name
```

```
            self.email: str = email
            self.phone: str = phone
            self.DOB: date = DOB

    def calculate_age(self) -> int:
        today = datetime.now().date()
        if (today.month, today.day) < (self.DOB.month, self.DOB.day):
            age = today.year - self.DOB.year - 1
        else:
            age = today.year - self.DOB.year
        return age

if __name__ == '__main__':
    c = Contact(
        "John Doe",
        "johndoe@example.com",
        "555-555-5555",
        date(1990, 1, 1))
    print(c.calculate_age())
```

Looking through this code, you can read exactly what you need to know about the arguments and returned values. In the init method of the Contact class you'll notice the arguments have been typecast. Also notice in the age method there is what looks like a right arrow. This is saying the returned value will be an int type. Just looking through this code you can read exactly what you need to know about the arguments and returned values. You don't have to typecast every time, but it's really nice when you do! Most of the time you'll thank your future self will be grateful you used typecasting.

DECORATORS

You can alter the functionality of methods and functions using decorators (as well as other objects, but mainly methods and functions). The @ sign precedes the decorator's name in a decorator. For instance, a decorator is "@property". The "property" decorator's primary purpose in design is memory preservation. Consider a Class that has numerous properties. It can be difficult for your application to function if you keep all those properties in memory at run time. Depending on the attribute, you might only require some attributes at a particular point in the application.

Instead, you use the "@property" decorator to make an attribute appear like a method. The attribute is called like any other attribute with the "@property" decorator. However, at the backend, it functions like a method. The addition to the "decorator example" is shown below. The Contact class we just established in the previous step will be copied and modified to add "age" as an attribute (decorated method).

```
from datetime import date, datetime

class Contact:
    def __init__(self, name: str, email: str, phone: str, DOB: date):
        self.name: str = name
        self.email: str = email
        self.phone: str = phone
```

```
        self.DOB: date = DOB

    @property
    def age(self):
        return self.calculate_age()

    def calculate_age(self) -> int:
        today = datetime.now().date()
        if (today.month, today.day) < (self.DOB.month, self.DOB.day):
            age = today.year - self.DOB.year - 1
        else:
            age = today.year - self.DOB.year
        return age

if __name__ == '__main__':
    c = Contact("John Doe", "johndoe@example.com", "555-555-5555", date(1990,
1, 1))
    print(c.calculate_age())
    print(c.age)
```

We could alternatively move all of the code from calculate_age to age and remove the calculate_age function entirely.

 Note: Decorators are a powerful tool in Python and can be used for many purposes, such as logging, authentication, and memoization

CHAPTER 7 CHALLENGE:

For this exercise we're going to create an "Item" class. The Item class will have the following:

- The attributes item_type (str), and item_name (str) as required to create an instance.
- Optional attributes sku (str), and sales_price (int).
- A private attribute named "_vendor_skus" (list).
- A method "vendor_skus" with the property decorator.
- The methods "add_vendor_skus", and "remove_vendor_skus".

In the add_vendor_skus method check if the required argument "vendor_skus" (you'll have to add the argument to the add_vendor_skus method) is a list or not. Then add the argument accordingly.

Once done creating the class do the following:

- Create a couple of instances for the class with items of your choice.
- Create the "__str__" method (two underscores before and after) that returns a sentence with the name of the item and how much the item costs in dollars.
- Make sure to check if the sales_price is set or not (since it's an optional attribute).
- Add a couple of vendor sku's to the first item.

- Add one vendor sku as a string and then two more vendor sku's inside of a list.
- Make sure to check the type in your add_vendor_skus method.
- If the wrong type is passed as an argument print something that says the type is wrong and what type was actually passed in.

See the next pages for the solution.

 Note: One nifty trick some programs use for financials is to record all money in cents rather than dollars. So instead of 20.14 dollars in the program, it will be 2014 cents. This is a lot easier in some respects because you don't have to worry about floats. It can be a problem for others because you need to remember to convert the number every time you display it.

CHAPTER 7 SOLUTION

```python
class Item:
    def __init__(self, item_type: str, item_name: str, sku: str = None,
sales_price: int = None):
        self.item_type: str = item_type
        self.item_name: str = item_name
        self.sku: str = sku
        self.sales_price: int = sales_price
        self._vendor_skus: list = []


    @property
    def vendor_skus(self):
        return self._vendor_skus

    def add_vendor_skus(self, vendor_skus):
        if isinstance(vendor_skus, list):
            setattr(self, '_vendor_skus', self._vendor_skus + vendor_skus)
        elif isinstance(vendor_skus, str):
            self._vendor_skus.append(vendor_skus)
        else:
            print(f'''Vendor SKUs can only be strings or lists.
                Your sku was a {type(vendor_skus)}.''')

    def remove_vendor_skus(self, vendor_skus):
        self._vendor_skus.remove(vendor_skus)

    def __str__(self):
        if self.sales_price:
            sales_price_str = \
            f'${str(self.sales_price)[:-2]}.{str(self.sales_price)[-2:]}'
            return \
            f"{self.item_name} will cost the customer {sales_price_str}"
        else:
            return f"{self.item_name} has no sales price yet."
```

```python
def main():
    item_a = Item('Inventory', 'Item A', 'abc-123', 10034)
    item_a.add_vendor_skus('cba-456')
    item_a.add_vendor_skus(['another_vendor_sku', 'some_other_vendor_sku'])
    item_a.add_vendor_skus(1456)
    print(item_a.vendor_skus)
    print(item_a)
    item_b = Item('Non-Inventory', 'Item B', 'abc-124')
    print(item_b)

if __name__ == '__main__':
    main()
```

CHAPTER 8
Inheritance and Composition

INHERITANCE VS COMPOSITION

I'm going to bring up the argument of inheritance vs composition now. You won't really be able to use what I'm about to say for a little while, and you may not fully understand what I'm about to say. That's ok. My main point in bringing the argument up now is so you don't get tunnel vision with inheritance. As your projects get more complicated, you'll get upset with your code if you believe that inheritance is the best of the best in OOP. For example Odoo is the largest ERP platform built on Python. If you ever start working with Odoo's code you'll quickly learn that their inheritance is so complex it's nearly impossible to understand if you just read the code. I'm trying to help you avoid this trap. So as you learn about inheritance, realize it's a puzzle piece not the end goal.

There are two different ways people implement OOP (Object Oriented Programming). One is called inheritance (which I'm about to explain). The other way is called Composition which I'll explain after inheritance. Composition programming is considered the better of the two in most situations. But even composition will have some inheritance inside of it. In other words you can't avoid the concepts of inheritance because it's everywhere in Python. As a result you must learn it eventually. So I'll start with it so you can at least know what it's all about. Just know I'm going to steer you away from it later.

INHERITANCE

The full power of objects begins to manifest itself through inheritance. It's also the point at which things become incredibly chaotic and challenging to understand. Shapes are a traditional method of teaching inheritance (a Rectangle inherits a Square). We will utilize accounting-related terms as we are all familiar with them.

I will start by saying that you shouldn't think of inheritance in terms of a parent-child relationship. I fell into that trap and experienced a lot of frustration while attempting to apply the concepts to accounting objects. I discovered that comparing inheritance to nested spreadsheet functions was the most effective approach. You can think of inheriting a Class as nesting it inside a new Class.

We're going to create the document "class_inheritance.py" and put the following code in it:

```python
class Transaction:

    def __init__(
                self,
                doc_number,
                amount,
                ledger_account,
                transaction_type
        ):
        self.doc_number = doc_number
        self.amount = amount
        self.ledger_account = ledger_account
        self.transaction_type = transaction_type
        self.is_open = True # For delattr example's sake.

class Bill(Transaction):
    # Notice "self" isn't needed for these attributes:
    transaction_type = 'Bill'
    ledger_account = 'Accounts Payable'

    def __init__(self, doc_number, amount, vendor):
        # When you see "super" think "initiate"
        # So for this super think >>
        # initiate(
        #         ThisClass,
        #         FromInheritedClass
        #     ).__init__(
        #             arguments_for_inherited_class
        #     )
        super(
                Bill,
                self
            ).__init__(
                    doc_number,
                    amount,
                    self.ledger_account,
                    self.transaction_type
            )
        self.vendor = vendor

class Check(Transaction):
    transaction_type = 'Check'

    def __init__(self, check_number, amount, ledger_account, payee):
        super(Check, self).__init__(
                check_number,
                amount,
                ledger_account,
                self.transaction_type
        )
        self.payee = payee

    @property # Decorator that makes method below act like an attribute
```

```
    def check_number(self):
        print('I look like a Method but act like an Attribute')
        return self.doc_number


def main():
    check = Check(1001, 1200.00, 'Checking 7659', 'Bricks R Us')
    bill = Bill(20221456, 463.45, 'Roofer Supply Inc.')
    print(bill.doc_number)
    print(isinstance(check, Check))
    print(bill)
    print(check.check_number + 1) # Using attribute in math


if __name__ == '__main__':
    main()
```

Ok, ok, there is a lot to unpack here. Don't feel too worried if a lot of it is over your head right now. Try your best to stick with me.

The first thing is the "Transaction" class. We could say every general ledger movement in accounting is a transaction at its core. It doesn't matter what we do, they are all transactions. As such, we can use the "Transaction" class as the base class for all types of transactions we want to create in our accounting system.

In terms of classes, the Transaction one is relatively dull. We pass in some arguments that are assigned to attributes. We don't need to duplicate this code elsewhere as we are doing it here. Writing the least amount of code necessary to complete the task while being understandable should be a significant objective for every developer. Here, inheritance enables reusing code without copy-and-paste for developers.

Bill is the name of the second class we make. To indicate that we want to inherit (also known as a nest) the Transaction class inside the Bill class, we place the parentheses around the Transaction class and the Bill class.

In the Bill class, we add a few attributes before the init method. These are Class Attributes vs. Instance Attributes. The difference is the nature of the Class Attributes across all instances of the class. Class attributes should only be those that won't change independently of the instance. As long as a Bill is an instance of the "Bill Class," its "transaction type" in this example is always and exclusively a "Bill," and it will never be anything else. The same is true for Accounts Payable (think QuickBooks here where multiple AP accounts is considered bad practice).

SUPER

Think of the word "Initiate" when you use the word "Super" in Python. Until I adjusted the term in my mind, I used to get caught up on the word Super. When you use the super method, you instruct Python to start the nested class into the class you're currently programming in ("self"). With that, you must provide arguments for the nested class's (inherited) init function. You can only access the nested attributes and methods if you utilize super. In the above example we initiate the Transaction class inside of the Bill class.

CLASS METHOD DECORATOR

Another decorator I want you to be aware of is the "@classmethod" decorator. Usually you can only call methods from a class instance. But sometimes you may want to call a method directly from the class without making an instance. This is where you would use the "@classmethod". Inside of the Chapter08 folder create a new document named "class_method_example.py". You'll need the document to be in this location because we'll pull in classes we created above and add to their functionality. Put the following code into "class_method_example.py":

```python
from Chapter08.class_inheritance import Bill
from Chapter08.class_inheritance import Check

class BillPaymentCheck(Check):
    transaction_type = 'Bill Payment Check'

    def __init__(self, check_number, amount, ledger_account, payee):
        super(BillPaymentCheck, self).__init__(
                check_number,
                amount,
                ledger_account,
                payee
        )

    @classmethod
    def pay_bill(cls, check_number, amount, ledger_account, bill):
        assert isinstance(bill, Bill)
        if amount < bill.amount:
            bill_payment_check = cls(
                        check_number,
                        amount,
                        ledger_account,
                        bill.vendor
            )
            return (bill, bill_payment_check)
        elif amount == bill.amount:
            bill_payment_check = cls(
                        check_number,
                        amount,
                        ledger_account, bill.vendor)
            bill.is_open = False
            return (bill, bill_payment_check)
        else:
            bill_payment_check = cls(
                        check_number,
                        bill.amount,
                        ledger_account,
                        bill.vendor
                )
            bill.is_open = False
            return (bill, bill_payment_check)

def main():
    bill = Bill(20221456, 463.45, 'Roofer Supply Inc.')
```

```
    bill, bill_payment_check = BillPaymentCheck.pay_bill(
                                        1003,
                                        463.45,
                                        'Main Checking 4334',
                                        bill
                            )
    print(bill_payment_check.amount)
    print(bill.is_open) # Will return False

if __name__ == '__main__':
    main()
```

Look at the second line in the main function. Notice, we didn't create an instance of the BillPaymentCheck class before we called the pay_bill method. We called the method directly from the class "BillPaymentCheck". Also notice inside the BillPaymentCheck class method pay_bill we replaced the word "self" with "cls". This highlights a principle that the word "self" isn't special, it's just the standard used word. It can be replaced by any string. In this case, we use "cls" to represent "class". When using "@classmethod" you create the class instance inside the method itself. I use class methods a lot in my projects.

MULTIPLE INHERITANCE

We were just using single inheritance but Python also has Multiple Inheritance. Multiple Inheritance isn't found in all programming languages. It's when a class inherits from more than one class at a time. The syntax would be "class Child(Parent1, Parent2):". I'm not going to go in depth into multiple inheritance in this book, I'm just making you aware that you'll come across it in the wild.

CHAPTER 8 CHALLENGE

This exercise is going to be a challenge. I've shown you how to create a Transaction class then inherit the class in the Bill and Check classes. Your challenge is to take those lessons and do the following tasks:

- Create a Contact class and
- Create the Vendor and Customer class inheriting the Contact class.
- Create attributes that are common between customers and vendors in the Contact class.
- Add at least one unique attribute and method to both the Vendor and Customer class.
- Create one customer and one vendor instance.
- Put your code inside of the file "chapter_08_challenge.py"

See the next page for the solution or find it in "chapter_08_challenge_solution.py" in this book's resources.

CHAPTER 8 CHALLENGE SOLUTION

```
class Contact:
    def __init__(self, first_name, last_name, phone_number, email):
        self.first_name = first_name
```

```python
        self.last_name = last_name
        self.phone_number = phone_number
        self.email = email

class Vendor(Contact):
    contact_type = 'Vendor'

    def __init__(
                self,
                first_name,
                last_name,
                phone_number,
                email,
                vendors_customer_id
        ):
        super().__init__(first_name, last_name, phone_number, email)
        self.vendors_customer_id = vendors_customer_id

    def add_address(self, address):

        # Assert is a combined if statement with Error
        # If the Assert statement is false an Error is thrown
        # Assert isn't handling the error it's just catching them
        assert 'street' in address.keys()
        assert 'city' in address.keys()
        assert 'state' in address.keys()
        assert 'zip' in address.keys()

        # The setattr method is the best way to add attributes
        #  when you're not inside the __init__ method.
        setattr(self, 'address', address)


class Customer(Contact):
    contact_type = 'Customer'

    def __init__(
                self,
                first_name,
                last_name,
                phone_number,
                email,
                preferred_delivery_method
        ):
        super().__init__(first_name, last_name, phone_number, email)
        self.preferred_delivery_method = preferred_delivery_method

    def get_balance(self):
        # For now this isn't a working method it's just an example
        balance = 0
        return balance

def main():
```

```
vendor = Vendor(
    "John",
    "Doe",
    "555-555-5555",
    "john.doe@example.com",
    '2342'
)
address = {
    "street": "123 Main St.",
    "city": "Fakeville",
    "state": "FA",
    "zip": "12345"
}
vendor.add_address(address)
print(vendor.address['street'])
customer = Customer(
    "John",
    "Doe",
    "555-555-5555",
    "john.doe@example.com",
    "mail"
)
print(customer.get_balance())
print(vendor.address['state'])

if __name__ == '__main__':
    main()
```

In this solution I've introduced the "assert" keyword. I'm using it to make sure the address argument passed into the add_address method has key components. There are lots of different ways to make sure the specific keys are in a dictionary, this is just one example. I'll go in more depth on assert in the future.

I also didn't do much with the get_balance function in the Customer class. For now, I was just trying to add an additional function. In the future we'll create functions that get and add data to/from databases.

COMPOSITION...THE BETTER WAY

Instead of using a "is a" technique, Composition uses a "has a" approach. Whereas in Composition, a Vendor "had" a Contact, with inheritance, a Vendor "is" a Contact. Why is that relevant? Vendor and Contact would become one class if we let Vendor inherit from Contact. In other words, if the Contact class malfunctions, the Vendor class likewise malfunctions. Not a big issue unless you're four or five generations thick. For instance, if a Vendor inherits a Business, a Sales Rep, a Contact, etc., your code may break deeply and result in various unanticipated issues that are challenging to troubleshoot.

Thanks to composition, a vendor may have qualities for a company, an address, and a sales representative. The sales representative could then have the Contact and Address qualities. In this case, if the Address breaks, simply the Address breaks—not the Company or the Sales Rep. See how convenient that is? Making classes into other classes' components may require us to write more code. Yet, our code is far easier to comprehend, debug, and expand. The objective in development is not to make the code with the least amount of keystrokes. The object is to develop practical, reusable, and simple code to read and debug.

For this example I'm going to use the inheritance challenge we just did, but I'm going to write it in a composition type way. I'll put the example in Chapter 8 folder named "composition_example.py"

```python
class Address:
    def __init__(self, street: str, city: str, state: str, zip: str):
        self.street: str = street
        self.city: str = city
        self.state: str = state
        self.zip: str = zip

class Contact:
    def __init__(
            self,
            first_name: str,
            last_name: str,
            phone_number: str,
            email: str,
            address: str = None
        ):
        self.first_name: str = first_name
        self.last_name: str = last_name
        self.phone_number: str = phone_number
        self.email: str = email
        self.address: Address = address

class Vendor:
    contact_type = 'Vendor'

    def __init__(
            self,
            Vendors_customer_id: int,
            contact: Contact
        ):
        self.vendors_customer_id: int = vendors_customer_id
        self.contact: Contact = contact

class Customer:
    contact_type = 'Customer'

    def __init__(
            self,
            contact: Contact,
            preferred_delivery_method: str = None
        ):
        self.contact: Contact = contact
        self.preferred_delivery_method: str = preferred_delivery_method

    def get_balance(self) -> float:
```

```
            # For now this isn't a working method it's just an example
            balance = 0.0
            return balance

def main():
    vendor_address = Address(
        "123 Main St.",
        "Fakeville",
        "FA",
        "12345"
    )
    vendor_contact = Contact(
        "John",
        "Doe",
        "555-555-5555",
        "john.doe@example.com",
        vendor_address
    )
    vendor = Vendor('2342', vendor_contact)

    customer_contact = Contact(
        "Jim",
        "Buckle",
        "555-555-5556",
        "john.doe@example.com"
    )
    customer = Customer(
        customer_contact,
        "mail"
    )
    print(customer.get_balance())
    print(vendor.contact.address.state)

if __name__ == '__main__':
    main()
```

The variations are minute, as you can see. In an illustration, the Vendor has a Contact with an Address and a state attribute. While it appears to have more code, it is also easier to read and modify. We would only need to alter the Address if we wanted to update the Address. It's segregated into its own tiny section, which makes it simple to get it right. Also, this is quite readable. The difference might not seem like much for now, but trust me, as your projects grow, the readability can differ significantly.

You'll also note that I typecast the values. It significantly improves the code's readability. It adds a wonderful finishing touch that helps your code look tidy.

CHAPTER 9

Test Driven Development

Since Chapter 1, we have made significant progress. This chapter dramatically turns the corner. Test-driven development, or TDD, is the ideal method for writing high-quality code quickly. The process of TDD typically involves the following steps in order:

1. Write a test that defines the desired behavior of the code
2. Run the test to ensure failure (our code hasn't even been developed yet, so it should).
3. Write the code until the test passes.
4. Rerun the test to confirm that the code behaves as expected.
5. For the tests to continue passing, modify the code as necessary.

What I've found is most people learning to code do a hybrid version of TDD. Let's take accounting as an example. An accountant may start with some sort of sample data in a spreadsheet. The accountant will bring that data into their code and try to do something with it. He'll then test it with different iterations of data to make sure it works with lots of different scenarios. The testing (checking) to see if the code worked every time is usually done manually. In TDD an accountant can automate the testing and can use the tests over and over. Also in TDD an accountant can add different scenarios. When the code is updated the pre-built tests can make sure the updates didn't break the original working code.

TDD also forces the programmer to comprehend what the code is genuinely accomplishing. I won't lie; TDD is not always easy. However, chasing minor issues down the road is much more complex than writing your tests correctly the first time.

I haven't introduced you to testing yet because it's essential to first comprehend the expected outcomes of your code and have a grasp of objects and inheritance. Now that we've overcome that hurdle, testing becomes significantly more logical.

TESTS

We're going to start a new folder named "Chapter09". Create the file "transactions.py" inside the folder and add the code below. It would help if you recognized it all because we worked on all of it in the last chapter:

```python
class Transaction:

    def __init__(
            self,
            doc_number: str,
            amount: float,
            ledger_account: str,
            transaction_type: str
            ):
        self.doc_number: str = doc_number
        self.amount: float = amount
        self.ledger_account: str = ledger_account
        self.transaction_type: str = transaction_type


class Bill:
    transaction_type = 'Bill'
    ledger_account = 'Accounts Payable'

    def __init__(self,
                doc_number: str,
                amount: float,
                vendor: str
                ):
        self.transaction: Transaction = Transaction(
            doc_number,
            amount,
            self.ledger_account,
            self.transaction_type
        )
        self.vendor: str = vendor


class Check:
    transaction_type = 'Check'

    def __init__(self,
                check_number: str,
                amount: float,
                ledger_account: str,
                payee: str
                ):
        self.transaction: Transaction = Transaction(
            check_number,
            amount,
            ledger_account,
            self.transaction_type
        )
        self.payee: str = payee

    @property
    def check_number(self) -> str:
```

```
print('I look like a Method but act like an Attribute')
return self.transaction.doc_number
```

 Note: I didn't include a "main" statement or function in the file because we won't need one. Generally, a piece of code's main statement and function are contained in just one file. The first step of our entire program is that file. We have the classes and functions to run the application in every other file.

TEST FILES AND FOLDERS

We will now make our test directories and files. It's conventional and highly recommended (almost required) to start the names of directories and files containing tests by the name "tests". So we're going to create a directory (with an __init__.py file) named "tests". In the tests directory we're going to create the file "test_transactions.py". It's convention to call the name of the file the same as the file we're going to test with the word "test_" before it (again almost required).

We're going to start by importing the required classes we want to test. We'll start with "Transactions". Add the following code:

```
from Chapter09.transactions import Transaction, Bill, Check
import unittest

class TestTransaction(unittest.TestCase):
    def setUp(self):
        # Create a Transaction object to use in the tests
        self.transaction = Transaction(
            '123',
            100.00,
            'Test account',
            'Test Type'
        )

    def test_init(self):
        # Test the attributes of the Transaction object
        self.assertIsInstance(self.transaction, Transaction)
        self.assertEqual(self.transaction.doc_number, '123')
        self.assertEqual(self.transaction.amount, 100.00)
        self.assertEqual(self.transaction.ledger_account, 'Test account')
        self.assertEqual(self.transaction.transaction_type, 'Test Type')

class TestBill(unittest.TestCase):
    #Notice this test is a lot like TestTransaction
    def setUp(self):
        # Create a Transaction object to use in the tests
        self.bill = Bill('123', 100.00, 'Widget Co.')

    def test_init(self):
        # Test the attributes of the Transaction object
        self.assertIsInstance(self.bill, Bill)
        self.assertEqual(self.bill.transaction.doc_number, '123')
```

```python
        self.assertEqual(self.bill.transaction.amount, 100.00)
        self.assertEqual(
            self.bill.transaction.ledger_account,
            'Accounts Payable'
        )
        self.assertEqual(self.bill.transaction_type, 'Bill')


class TestCheck(unittest.TestCase):
    def setUp(self):
        # Create a Transaction object to use in the tests
        self.check = Check(
            '123',
            100.00,
            'Operating Checking',
            'Widget Co.'
        )

    def test_init(self):
        # Test the attributes of the Transaction object
        self.assertIsInstance(self.check, Check)
        self.assertEqual(self.check.transaction.doc_number, '123')
        self.assertEqual(self.check.check_number, '123')
        self.assertEqual(self.check.transaction.amount, 100.00)
        self.assertEqual(
            self.check.transaction.ledger_account,
            'Operating Checking'
        )
        self.assertEqual(self.check.transaction_type, 'Check')
```

> **Note:** When attempting to use Pycharm's Debugging features while running a test, you may notice that the program won't halt if a breakpoint (red dot) is placed inside the setUp method. To make the breakpoint work, place it inside methods other than setUp. Combining Pycharm's Debugger with TDD's programming style can be quite useful.

We'll begin by constructing the "TestTransaction" class, which inherits from the "unittest.TestCase" class. Instead of using an init method for class initialization, we employ a special "setUp" method to prepare the tests. Within the setUp method, we utilize the code as we would expect to in the actual "do something" section of our program. Previously, we used the main function and created pseudo-tests within it. Rather than continuing this approach, we will incorporate that portion of the code into the "setUp" method. In this instance, we're generating a transaction and adding it to self.transaction.

The "test transaction attributes" method only checks to verify if an instance was indeed created and if the arguments we gave to the class were placed in the appropriate attributes. To check the instance first, we're using the assertIsInstance function. The tests you run will nearly always consist of assertSomething methods. Below are some examples of some of the methods available:

assertEqual	assertTrue	assertIsInstance	assertIs
assertIsNot	assertFalse	assertAlmostEqual	assertRaises
assertGreater	assertLess	assertGreaterEqual	assertLessEqual
assertIn	assertRegex	assertCountEqual	assertRaises

I've included a few basic tests above to pique your interest. If I were concerned about other potential issues, I might introduce various data types into the Transaction class arguments and conduct an assertRaises test to ensure my code can handle them. If there were additional methods, I would test each one to verify that the returned results align with my expectations for a range of arguments.

THE FLOW OF DEVELOPING THE TDD WAY

In reality, we might have a spreadsheet with test results. Let's start by looking for the most basic case in the test data. If needed, we may need to make up a very simple fictitious example. At this point, the question "what are we supposed to test?" arises. There is no set formula for what must be tested and what must not. I recommend testing classes, methods, and functions.

- Test classes to make sure they are initiated and attributes are added properly.
- Test methods and functions to make sure the returns are what you want and/or the expected changes happened like you expected.

Let's say we had a spreadsheet with expenses. The expense types are bills, credit card charges, checks, and journals. For the sake of education, let's say all we want to do is make sure we import them into our code correctly and make sure we categorize the type correctly. You're internal dialog should go something like this:

"I need to import the transactions. Let's write a function that imports the transactions."
"First I'll create a TestImportTransactions class with a Setup method."
"How do I want to use the code?"
"In Setup I'll write a line like: self.transactions = import_transactions() because that's how I want to use this function."
"import_transactions function doesn't exist so I'll create a file and add the function in the file."
"In the import_transactions function I'll add one line with 'pass' in it, just to get it started."
"When I run import_transactions what do I want the transactions to be in Python?"
"Maybe a List or a Dictionary?"
"Let's make it a List of Lists."
"After the Setup method I'll create test_import_transactions method."
"First test is to see if what I just imported is actually a list type."
"Add self.assertIsInstance(self.transactions, list)."
"Now I'll run the test… Test failed…Perfect!"
"Now I'll add code to the import_transactions function and keep running the test until it passes."

You'll keep up a dialog like this until you have a bunch of tests checking a bunch of scenarios you can think of that might break your code. As you're developing, you're only trying to develop enough code to pass your tests. The point is, once you have those tests built, and they all pass, there is a much lower chance your program will break in the wild. Also you won't be developing unnecessary code because all you're trying to do is pass the test you created.

CHAPTER 9 EXERCISE:

For this exercise we're going to create a directory (folder with no init file) inside the Chapter09 directory named "chapter_09_exercise". Create two files in the chapter_09_exercise directory named "journal_entry.py" and "test_journal_entry.py". Like I've mentioned before, you'll usually put test files inside test folders. However, with a simple 1 file project, it's fine keeping some simplicity and adding the test file in the same hierarchy.

We'll start inside journal_entry and we'll create a very simple class named "JournalEntry" with the following code:

```
class JournalEntry:
    pass
```

Throughout this exercise, I'll be highlighting the aspects we need. Our first step is to create a failing test. Once we've done that, we'll expand the JournalEntry class's functionality until our tests pass. I'll document my thoughts and observations step by step as I progress through the process, allowing you to follow along. As I outline our needs and create the tests, I encourage you to try implementing the functionality yourself and achieve a passing test before examining my solution. While there isn't always a right or wrong way to develop code, there are certainly ways to create code that simply doesn't work, which we aim to avoid.

For this exercise, we'll employ type casting and construct our objects using a composition methodology instead of inheritance. Please note that I'm demonstrating my current approach to TDD. There are others who have developed alternative methods, and I encourage you to explore various ways people approach TDD.

Inside "test_journal_entry.py" add the following code to get us started

```
import unittest
from Chapter09.chapter_09_exercise.journal_entry import JournalEntry as JE

class TestJournalEntry(unittest.TestCase):

    def setUp(self):
        self.je = JE()

    def test_init(self):
        pass
```

 Note: I've abbreviated JournalEntry as JE, which is acceptable because accountants frequently refer to journals as JEs. As a general guideline, we should only use acronyms if they are widely recognized within the industry. We shouldn't create unique acronyms that only exist in our code and are only comprehensible to those who examine our code. The code should be easily readable by anyone familiar with the accounting industry and proficient in Python.

The first step is to test that the provided arguments are correctly assigned to the appropriate attributes. Consider the attributes a journal entry might have, and write tests to ensure self.je has those attributes, keeping in mind that the tests will initially fail.

Here are the initial tests I'll be adding to test_journal_attributes:

```python
self.assertIsInstance(self.je, JE)
self.assertEqual(self.je.journal_id, '1')
self.assertEqual(self.je.date, '12/31/2022')
self.assertIsNotNone(self.je.lines)
```

Upon running the test, I receive an error stating, "AttributeError: 'JournalEntry' object has no attribute 'journal_id'". I anticipate encountering the same errors with other attributes, so let's enhance the JournalEntry class to pass the current test as-is.

Try to implement this on your own before examining my solution.

Instead of presenting the entire code with each modification, I'll only display the pertinent code I'm adding. For our JournalEntry class, I'll introduce an init method and the capability to accept some arguments.

```python
def __init__(self, journal_id, date, lines):
    self.journal_id: str = journal_id
    self.date: str = date
    self.lines: list = lines
```

If I run the test again I'll get the following error: TypeError: JournalEntry.__init__() missing 3 required positional arguments: 'journal_id', 'date', and 'lines'

I need to pass those arguments when I create the journal so I'll change the setUp method in TestJournalEntry to add the relative data.

```python
def setUp(self):
    self.je = JE('1', '12/31/2022', [])
```

After I run the test again, I get the "OK" response (which means my tests passed). Wait What??? That doesn't look right. I didn't add any lines to the journal, right? Does it make sense (as an accountant) to have a journal with no lines in it? No it doesn't. So let's test to make sure there are at least two lines in the journal. In test_je_attributes I'll add the following test:

```python
self.assertEqual(len(self.je.lines), 2)
```

The test now fails with the error "AssertionError: 0 != 2". The Traceback section of the error report indicates the line where the error occurred. By examining the code in Pycharm, I can see that the line in question is the test I just added.

I need two lines, but how should they be structured? As a dictionary? Classes? A tuple? I believe the lines should be contained within a list, so let's add a test for that. Moreover, I want to confirm that it's a list before checking that there are two lines. If the lines are not a list, the len function in my test won't function properly.

```
self.assertIsInstance(self.je.lines, list)
```

Inside the list, I want each item to be an instance of the Line class.

```
for line in self.je.lines:
        self.assertIsInstance(line, JE_Line)
```

My test will still not pass because I haven't added any lines into the setUp method. But more importantly I don't even have a Line class. For simplicity, I'm going to create the Line class inside "journal_entry.py" with the following code:

```
class JournalEntryLine:
    pass
```

Back to the TestJournalEntry setUp method, I need to create a list of JE Lines in order to make sure I can pass my current test error (2 != 0). First, I'll import the JournalEntryLine class into "test_journal_entry.py".

```
from Chapter09.chapter_09_exercise.journal_entry import JournalEntryLine as JE_Line
```

I'll then change setUp to look like this:

```
def setUp(self):
        line_1 = JE_Line()
        line_2 = JE_Line()
        self.je = JE('1', '12/31/2022', [line_1, line_2])
```

 Note: Typically, using labels like "_1" and "_2" in code is considered bad practice. However, in tests, it makes sense to use them for reference purposes.

After running the test again, it passes! However, we're not quite done yet. Although the test has passed, we know that there are still aspects that require testing. For instance, we've created a new class (JournalEntryLine) that needs to be tested.

We'll add the test for JournalEntryLine within "test_journal_entry.py," above TestJournalEntry. The reason for placing it above is that we want to test the components before testing the main entity. In this case, JournalEntryLine is one of the components, and JournalEntry is the main element. Below is the beginning of TestJournalEntryLine. I used some logic to determine what fields a journal line would require and what sample amounts could be. If you have existing data, this would be an opportune moment to utilize it.

```python
class TestJournalEntryLine(unittest.TestCase):

    def setUp(self):
        self.je_line = JE_Line()

    def test_init(self):
        self.assertIsInstance(self.je_line, JE_Line)
        self.assertEqual(self.je_line.line_id, '1')
        self.assertEqual(self.je_line.account, 'Petty Cash')
        self.assertEqual(self.je_line.description, 'Cash For Sale')
        self.assertEqual(self.je_line.debit, 100.00)
        self.assertEqual(self.je_line.credit, 0)
        self.assertIsNotNone(self.je_line.journal_id)
```

 Note: While developing a specific test, it can be useful to comment out other tests. For example, while we're working on TestJournalEntryLine, we may choose to comment out TestJournalEntry. This might not be important right now, but in the future, when you have many tests that you don't want to run every time, it could be significant.

When we run TestJournalEntryLine, we encounter the error "AttributeError: 'JournalEntryLine' object has no attribute 'line_id'". This was anticipated, and we can expect similar errors for the other attributes as well. Let's proceed with completing the JournalEntryLine, enabling it to accept the correct attributes.

```python
class JournalEntryLine:

    def __init__(
            self,
            journal_id,
            line_id,
            account,
            amount,
            description=None,
            is_debit=True
    ):
        self.journal_id: int = journal_id
        self.line_id: int = line_id
        self.account: str = account
        self.description: str = description
        if is_debit:
            self.debit = amount
            self.credit = 0
        else:
            self.debit = 0
            self.credit = amount
```

While building out the class, I thought of a way to make sure there is an amount in only one side of the debit/ credit columns so I added the capability. Now I'm going to change the setUp method to create the object with its new capability. Below is my new setUp method:

```
def setUp(self):
    self.je_line = JE_Line(1, 1, 'Petty Cash', 100, 'Cash For Sale', True)
```

I've chosen to change the line_id to an integer rather than a string (The line_id was a str in the JournalEntry class). For consistency, I'll also modify the JournalEntry journal_id attribute to an integer. To ensure I don't forget to make this change later, I'll update the test_je_attributes line that checks the journal_id. If I forget to make the change to JournalEntry later, my test will trigger an error and remind me. The updated line will look like this:

```
self.assertEqual(self.je.journal_id, 1)
```

I also need to change the line_id test in test_je_line_attributes from str '1' to an int 1.

```
self.assertEqual(self.je_line.line_id, 1)
```

By running only TestJournalEntryLine (with TestJournalEntry commented out), the test now passes. Examining TestJournalEntry, I notice that I need to update the setUp method's line_1 and line_2 with more details. I'll modify the setUp method as follows:

```
def setUp(self):
    line_1 = JE_Line(1, 1, 'Petty Cash', 100, 'Cash For Sale', True)
    line_2 = JE_Line(1, 2, 'Sales', 100, 'Sale', False)
    self.je = JE(1, '12/31/2022', [line_1, line_2])
```

Take note that I've also changed the JE's id to an integer, ensuring that it will pass as well. Now, when I run both tests, everything passes.

I'll conclude the exercise at this point. If I were to continue, I would test other aspects, such as a third line, checking if JEs are balanced, altering amounts so they don't balance and verifying that it fails, and testing line_ids for duplicates and ensuring they fail when duplicates are present. I would also attempt to add amounts to the credit when amounts already exist in the debit of a je_line to ensure it didn't work. None of these tests would pass initially. I would then write the necessary code until they did pass.

The main idea is that, after considering various ways to break the code and testing those scenarios in official tests, there's a high likelihood that your code won't break post-deployment. If it does break at some point, gather the details of the input data and create a test for it. Adjust the code to pass the test, and then run all the tests. This will ensure that any modifications you've made won't break previous code. Consequently, when you re-deploy, the code will be more robust and well-tested.

SECTION 3

SQL AND DATA

It's impossible to discuss Python without touching upon SQL. Although you don't need to be a Database Administrator, understanding how to create queries and integrate them into your code is crucial, particularly when using ODBC connectors to interface with data. As such, this book will briefly delve into some SQL principles. However, we'll only focus on the essentials you truly need to know.

CHAPTER 10

DBeaver

I believe that learning SQL is best done separately from Python. Therefore, we'll momentarily set aside our Python focus and put on our data hat. To help with this, we're going to introduce a new, free, and user-friendly tool called DBeaver.

DOWNLOAD AND INSTALL

If you go to *https://dbeaver.io/* you can download the community edition of DBeaver. I find the community edition plenty for our needs. Installing the program is pretty straight forward. I suggest using all defaults except you'll want to select "Associate .SQL files" when given the chance in the select components screen.

PROJECTS

Inside DBeaver the left column is the Projects pane. The default project is usually "General". Inside the General project you usually have "Connections", "Scripts", and other tabs we won't discuss. Inside the "Scripts" folder are your SQL files. See figure 10.1.

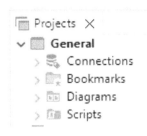

Figure 10.1

CREATE SQLITE DATABASE

In the menu bar click on "Database" then "New Database Connection". See figure 10.2.

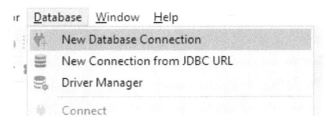

In the "Select your database" window choose "SQLite". See figure 10.3.

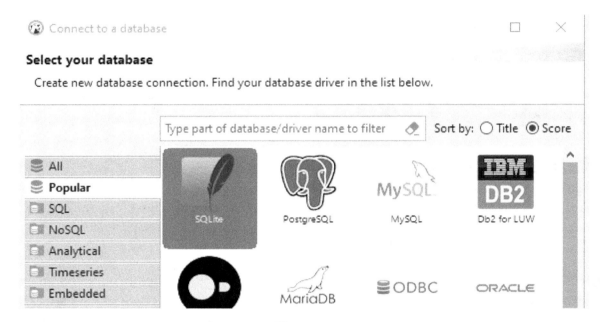

Figure 10.3

In the "Connect to a database" window select "Create". See figure 10.4.

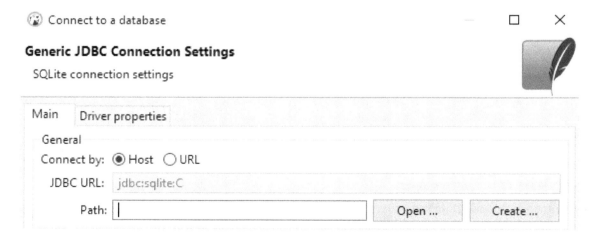

Figure 10.4

In the "file name" box, type "chapter10.db" as the database name. Click "Save", then back in the "Connect to a database" window, click "Finish". What you've done is create an SQLite Database.

CREATE NEW SQL SCRIPT
In the menu bar, click "SQL Editor" and then "New SQL Script". See figure 10.5.

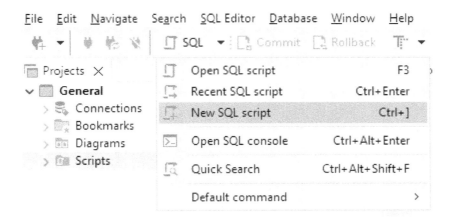

Figure 10.5

In the new script you can right click on the name of the script and then select "Rename File" to rename the script to "chapter10_script". See figure 10.6.

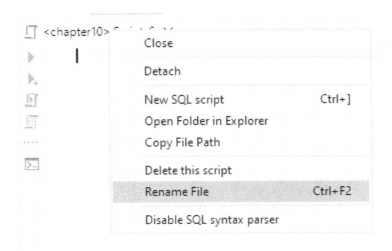

Figure 10.6

CHAPTER 11

SQL Basics

Although SQL differs from database to database, there are certain similarities. You may utilize joins differently or various datatypes in some databases. Here, I will provide the fundamentals so you can use Google to ask the correct queries. It's similar to comparing spreadsheet technologies to compare database technologies. You can utilize Google Sheets and Numbers if you know the basics of Excel. Although they vary, they are all essentially the same.

CREATE TABLE

I'm going to start with the create table section. Most of the time you'll already have a database to work with. If you don't you can usually create one from the UI of most SQL tools. The create table statement does just that, creates tables. Here is the basic syntax for the create table statement:

```
CREATE TABLE table_name (
    column1_name data_type constraint,
    column2_name data_type constraint,
    ...
    constraint
);
```

- "table_name" is the name of the table you want to create.
- "column1_name", "column2_name", etc. are the names of the columns in the table.
- "data_type" can be different depending on the database technology.
- "constraint" are rules that should be applied to the column (e.g. NOT NULL, UNIQUE, PRIMARY KEY, etc.).

> **Note:** If you come from other database systems such as MySQL and PostgreSQL, you notice that they use static typing. It means when you declare a column with a specific data type, it can only store data of the declared data type.

But SQLite is different from other database systems. SQLite uses a dynamic type system. In other words, a value stored in a column determines its data type, not the column's data type.

Here are 5 storage classes in SQLite:

Storage Class	Meaning
NULL	NULL values mean missing information or unknown.
INTEGER	Integer values are whole numbers (either positive or negative). An integer can have variable sizes such as 1, 2,3, 4, or 8 bytes.
REAL	Real values are real numbers with decimal values that use 8-byte floats.
TEXT	TEXT is used to store character data. The maximum length of TEXT is unlimited. SQLite supports various character encodings.
BLOB	BLOB stands for a binary large object that can store any kind of data. The maximum size of BLOB is, theoretically, unlimited.

Earlier in the book we created the Transaction class. We will revisit that class but assume this is our new code optimized:

```
class Transaction:

    def __init__(
            self,
            id: int,
            amount: float,
            ledger_account: str,
            transaction_type: str
            ):
        self.id: int = id
        self.amount: float = amount
        self.ledger_account: str = ledger_account
        self.transaction_type: str = transaction_type
```

The question is, how do we create a matching table? Below is the sql that would create this table:

```
CREATE TABLE transactions (
    id INTEGER PRIMARY KEY,
    amount REAL NOT NULL,
    ledger_account TEXT NOT NULL,
    transaction_type TEXT NOT NULL
);
```

Let's analyze this statement. I'm creating a table named "transactions" with the first column being "id" as an "integer". Capitalized words aren't always necessary, as most modern tools will correct the case and run the query just fine. The combination of "id integer" is the only required part of the second line. The constraint "PRIMARY KEY" isn't technically necessary, but I included it here for the sake of good database design.

As an accountant, you'll often start with a CSV file or Excel file containing all the data. In such situations, you might not add the primary key. In SQLite, primary key fields start at one and auto-increment by +1 for each subsequent primary key. This is why, if you're importing data into the table and it already has an id, you may want to skip the primary key constraint.

The "amount" column is of the "real" type, which is SQLite's equivalent of Python's Float type. Both types allow for decimal values. It's worth noting that for large projects, integers store data more efficiently and perform faster than real/float types. This is another reason you might want to represent money as cents rather than dollars. The "Not Null" constraint ensures that the column must contain a value. Null represents the absence of value. It's important to note that it's not an empty string or zero; it is Null.

Also, pay close attention to the semicolon (";") at the end of the statement. In SQL, if you don't include the semicolon, your statement is not considered complete. This means it either won't run or will run with the lines following it.

In DBeaver, add the code above in the script area and execute the statement. You can run the statement by placing your cursor anywhere in the code and pressing Ctrl+Enter, clicking the orange play symbol (without the plus sign), or going to SQL Editor > Execute SQL Statement. Refer to Figure 11.1.

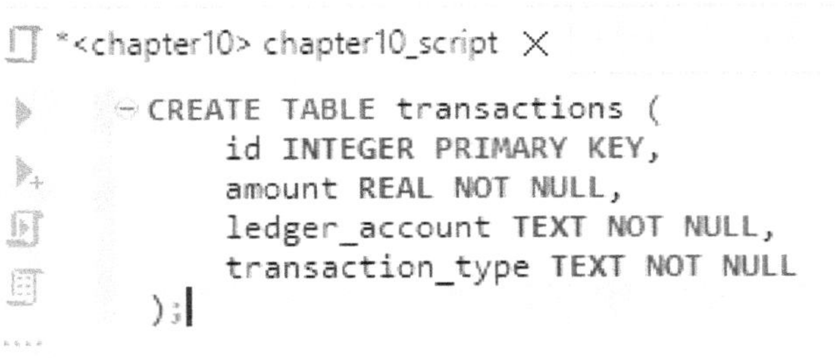

```
*<chapter10> chapter10_script  X

  CREATE TABLE transactions (
      id INTEGER PRIMARY KEY,
      amount REAL NOT NULL,
      ledger_account TEXT NOT NULL,
      transaction_type TEXT NOT NULL
  );
```

Figure 11.1

After running the code, you should get a popup on the bottom of DBeaver that gives you confirmation the code was run. See figure 11.2.

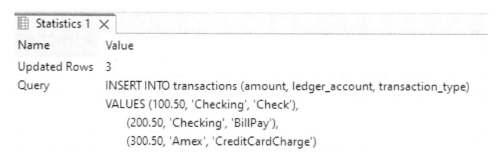

Figure 11.2

INSERT

Now that we have our table, we can begin adding data. We do this by using the INSERT statement. You can add one or more rows at a time with the insert statement. Below is the basic syntax for an insert statement.

```
INSERT INTO table_name (column1, column2, column3, ...) VALUES (value1,
value2, value3, ...);
```

It's important to start with the phrase "INSERT INTO," followed by the table name. Although capitalization may not be crucial in other parts of the statement, table names, column names, and values are all case-sensitive. In SQL, "Transactions" and "transactions" are considered distinct entities. Here's how I would insert three different transactions into the transactions table. Place this code below the create table code. Keep in mind that when you run the code in this script, only the code where your cursor is located will be executed.

```
INSERT INTO transactions (amount, ledger_account, transaction_type)
VALUES (100.50, 'Checking', 'Check'),
       (200.50, 'Checking', 'BillPay'),
       (300.50, 'Amex', 'CreditCardCharge');
```

It's important to note that in this insert statement, the "id" column is not used. SQLite will automatically populate the "id" column in the table as data is inserted. Another thing to observe is that strings are enclosed in single quotes rather than double quotes. Execute the above code, and you should see something similar to Figure 11.3 at the bottom of DBeaver.

Figure 11.3

SELECT

Now that there is data in the table, you can perform select queries, which are the essence of SQL. The first thing to understand is that the asterisk symbol (*) is a wildcard used to select all. The most basic query is "SELECT * FROM table_name;". Give it a try, and you'll see that you get all the data from the table. Here is an example of the code:

```
select * from transactions;
```

I received every row from the transactions table in response. See figure 11.4.

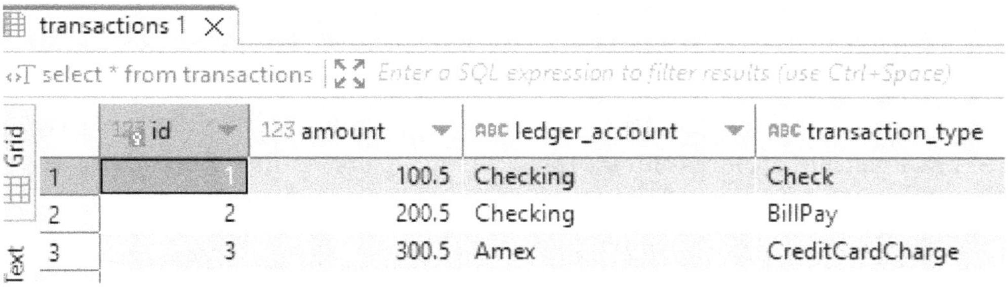

Figure 11.4

Here are some other queries you should try to get a feel of how select works. Notice these queries are fairly impractical but are mainly demonstration purposes.

```
select amount, transaction_type from transactions;
select *, id from transactions;
select transaction_type, id from transactions;
```

WHERE

Queries become more interesting when you add WHERE clauses. The WHERE clause can be added to SELECT, UPDATE, and DELETE queries. The syntax is added after the main part of your statement. For example, if the query is "SELECT * FROM transactions;", the WHERE clause should be added after the table name 'transactions' but before the semicolon. The syntax is "WHERE column_name operator criteria". Here are some examples to consider. Run each query and try to understand why each query produces the results it does.

```
select * from transactions where ledger_account = 'Checking';
select * from transactions where amount > 150;
select * from transactions where id not in (2);
select * from transactions where transaction_type like '%Card%';
select * from transactions where transaction_type like 'Card%';
select * from transactions where transaction_type like 'Credit%';
select * from transactions where transaction_type like '%Charge';
select * from transactions
    where ledger_account = 'Checking'
        and amount > 150;
```

```
select * from transactions
    where ledger_account = 'Checking'
        or amount > 150;
```

 Note: The spacing makes no difference in the function of the code like it does in Python. However, it's sometimes a good idea to add spacing for the sake of readability.

Here are some operators that can be used: =, <>, <, >, <=, >=, BETWEEN, LIKE, IN, IS NULL, and IS NOT NULL

UPDATE

Updating a record requires a WHERE clause. Without a WHERE clause, every row in the table will be updated. One way to ensure that your UPDATE statement is correct is to first use a SELECT statement with a WHERE clause. If the SELECT statement returns only the rows you want to update, then you know your WHERE clause works for that particular dataset (though it doesn't guarantee it will work for all datasets).

The syntax for an UPDATE statement is: "UPDATE table_name SET column_name = new_value where_clause".

For example, if you want to update a transaction amount from its current value to a different value, your query might look like this:

```
Update transactions set amount = 151 where id = 2;
```

To check and make sure the update worked as expected we would add the same where clause to the end of a select statement:

```
select * from transactions where id = 2;
```

We can also do some math inside of our update and other statements. Consider the following statement:

```
update transactions set amount = (amount + 1) where id = 2;
```

DELETE

It's important to be cautious when using the DELETE statement, as there usually isn't an undo button. It's best to avoid using DELETE unless absolutely necessary. When you do need to use it, make sure to perfect the WHERE clause using a SELECT statement first, and then apply the WHERE clause to the DELETE statement. Every rookie inevitably forgets this step and accidentally deletes everything in their table. Aim to make this mistake on something other than a production database.

The syntax for a DELETE statement is: "DELETE FROM table_name where_clause;". Consider the following example DELETE statements, where each transaction is deleted one at a time:

```
delete from transactions where id = 2;
delete from transactions
    where ledger_account = 'Checking'
        and amount < 150;
delete from transactions where amount > 150;
```

Now you can go back to the original insert statement and run it to add the transactions back in.

AGGREGATE FUNCTIONS

Aggregate functions operate on a set of rows and return a single result. The SELECT statement often uses Aggregate functions with GROUP BY and HAVING clauses. You should be pretty familiar with aggregate functions since they are basically the same as what's in Excel.

SQLite provides the following aggregate functions:

- AVG() – returns the average value of a group.
- COUNT() – returns the number of rows that match a specified condition
- MAX() – returns the maximum value in a group.
- MIN() – returns the minimum value in a group
- SUM() – returns the sum of values

```
select count(*) from transactions;
select max(amount) from transactions;
select min(amount) from transactions;
select sum(amount) from transactions;
select avg(amount) from transactions;
```

NESTED

The last thing I want to touch on is the nested statement. Nesting statements will feel a lot like nested Excel functions and are wildly powerful. Consider the below statements and you can get a sense of how they could be really helpful.

```
delete from transactions where id in
    (select id from transactions where amount > 150);
```

## CHAPTER 12

SQL In Python

SQL can be useful by itself, but it's most useful when you can combine it with a general programming language like Python. I'm going to show you the basics of how to connect to a few popular databases and how to include sql in your code.

SQL can be helpful, but combining it with a general programming language like Python is most beneficial. I will show you the basics of connecting to a few popular databases and how to include SQL in your code.

POPULAR LIBRARIES

To use SQL in Python, you can use a variety of libraries and modules that provide database connectivity and query execution. Some of the most commonly used libraries for SQL in Python are:

- SQLite: As mentioned earlier, SQLite is a lightweight, embedded relational database management system that is built into Python. It provides a simple way to store and retrieve data from a database file, without the need for a separate server process.
- SQLAlchemy: SQLAlchemy is a popular SQL toolkit and Object-Relational Mapping (ORM) library for Python that provides a high-level SQL abstraction layer. It supports multiple SQL dialects, including SQLite, MySQL, PostgreSQL, and Oracle.
- PyMySQL: PyMySQL is a pure-Python MySQL client library that provides a simple way to connect to a MySQL database and execute SQL statements.
- Psycopg2: Psycopg2 is a PostgreSQL adapter for Python that provides a way to connect to a PostgreSQL database and execute SQL statements.

I'm not going to go into depth with any one library, I'm just trying to point you in the right direction.

CONNECTION AND CURSOR

Working with databases in Python can be thought of as stepping into a building and stepping back out. You wouldn't try to enter another building without first stepping out of the current one. The same applies to connecting with databases: once you connect to a database, make sure to disconnect after you're done working with it. We'll start by connecting to SQLite, as it's the easiest to work with. SQLite has no users or permissions, and you control access to the database by managing access to the folder containing the database file. This makes SQLite popular for mobile app development since only users with access to the phone's folders can access the database. It's also a great starting point for learning databases, as you don't need to worry about additional security protocols and server management.

Below is the basic code to connect, query, iterate through results, and disconnect from an SQLite database. You'll find the code in the "Chapter12" folder inside "sqlite_connection.py".

```python
import sqlite3

def main():
    # Connect to the database (or create it if it doesn't exist)
    conn = sqlite3.connect(r"""
C:\Users\selfjared\Documents\PythonProjects\AccountingPy\Chapter12\chapter12.
db""""
    )
    cursor = conn.cursor()

    # create the table to query
    cursor.execute("""
        CREATE TABLE transactions (
            id INTEGER PRIMARY KEY,
            amount REAL NOT NULL,
            ledger_account TEXT NOT NULL,
            transaction_type TEXT NOT NULL
        );
    """)

    # Insert the data to query
    cursor.execute("""
        INSERT INTO transactions (amount, ledger_account, transaction_type)
        VALUES (100.50, 'Checking', 'Check'),
               (200.50, 'Checking', 'BillPay'),
               (300.50, 'Amex', 'CreditCardCharge');
    """)

    # query the data
    cursor.execute("SELECT * FROM transactions")
    results = cursor.fetchall()
    for row in results:
        print(row)

    # Close the connection
    conn.close()

if __name__ == '__main__':
    main()
```

The cursor object provides the execute method, which enables you to run SQL code. When the code is executed, the database sends a response back to the cursor. To retrieve the data from the cursor/database, you use the fetchall() method in the cursor. After that, you can iterate through the results. In technical terms, the results are a list, and the rows are tuples. We've covered similar data structures in the past, so this concept should not be entirely new.

IMPORTING FROM LIST OF TUPLES

When working with data in Python, you'll often encounter a list of tuples. This structure is useful because tuples are immutable, ensuring that the content of a specific column remains consistent across all tuples. This is also the format in which select query results are returned. If you have a list of tuples and want to import them into a database, you can use the following basic script as a reference. Check out the file "list_of_tuples.py" in Chapter 12 for more details.

```python
import sqlite3

def main():
    # Connect to the database (or create it if it doesn't exist)
    conn = sqlite3.connect(r'''C:\Users\selfjared\Documents\PythonProjects\
AccountingPy\Chapter12\chapter12.db''')
    cursor = conn.cursor()

    # create the table to query
    cursor.execute('''
        CREATE TABLE IF NOT EXISTS transactions_from_list_of_tuples (
        id INTEGER PRIMARY KEY,
        amount REAL NOT NULL,
        ledger_account TEXT NOT NULL,
        transaction_type TEXT NOT NULL
        );
    ''')

    transactions = [
        (100.50, 'Checking', 'Check'),
        (200.50, 'Checking', 'BillPay'),
        (300.50, 'Amex', 'CreditCardCharge')
    ]
    # Insert the data to query
    cursor.executemany('''
        INSERT INTO transactions (amount, ledger_account, transaction_type)
        VALUES (?, ?, ?);
    ''', transactions)

    # query the data
    cursor.execute("SELECT * FROM transactions")
    results = cursor.fetchall()
    for row in results:
        print(row)

    # Close the connection
    conn.close()

if __name__ == '__main__':
    main()
```

Notice I also changed the create table statement to include "if not exists". This is another handy code to keep around if you're going to be deleting information and testing it a bunch of times. Sometimes you just don't want to deal with errors if the table exists and don't want to deal with creating the table if it doesn't.

ODBC BASICS

ODBC stands for Open Database Connectivity, and it is a standard API for accessing relational databases. The primary goal of this chapter is to provide you with the essential knowledge needed to work with most ODBC connectors. Although most ODBC connectors do support SQL join statements, this book will not cover them. That said, joins indeed play a significant role in SQL, and you should research the topic further.

ODBC connectors serve as universal gateways that allow you to manipulate and extract data in various programs. For instance, if you want to delete every invoice in the clearing account with a value greater than $500, you can simply pass the query "delete from Invoices where amount > 500;". This kind of functionality can save you a considerable amount of time and effort.

Each ODBC connector has its own way of doing things. The first thing to understand is that there are 32-bit and 64-bit connectors. You need to know which one you're trying to connect to in order to make a successful connection. You'll hopefully know by the DSN (Data Source Name). If you have the same DSN for a 32-bit and a 64-bit connector, you'll want to change the DSN of one of them to avoid confusion.

If you're connecting Python to an ODBC connection, the following is a sample script you can use:

```
import pyodbc

dsn = 'mydsn'
user = 'myuser'
password = 'mypassword'

cnxn = pyodbc.connect(f'DSN={dsn};UID={user};PWD={password}')
cursor = cnxn.cursor()

# Execute a query
cursor.execute("SELECT * FROM mytable")

# Fetch all the results
results = cursor.fetchall()

# Close the cursor and connection
cursor.close()
cnxn.close()
```

Making the cnxn doesn't need to be complicated. For some ODBC connections, you can use the "Test Connection" feature directly from the ODBC Connection screen (double-click on the connection in the "ODBC Data Source Administrator" window). If you get a success screen, you don't have to pass the user and password variables into the connection. In that situation, you can replace the cnxn line above with the following simplified line:

```
cnxn = pyodbc.connect(f'DSN={your_dsn}')
```

This makes the connection process more streamlined and efficient.

CHAPTER 13

Pandas

Pandas is an incredibly powerful Python library that can be used for data manipulation, analysis, and visualization. Once you get the hang of using pandas, you may wonder why you ever relied on spreadsheets. This book cannot cover the entire scope of pandas, but it will provide you with the basics you need to avoid frustration when working with it. The syntax may seem a bit unusual at first, but with practice, you'll become more comfortable. Pandas is particularly useful for wholesale data manipulation as opposed to individual transactions.

PANDAS VS OBJECTS

The question of when to use pandas and when to invest in creating objects for each data line can be challenging to answer. If you need to make decisions about individual transactions, such as retrieving shipping dates from a third-party software based on the order ID, creating objects for your data might be the better option. However, if you can extract data from one source, make some adjustments while keeping the data mostly intact, and then load it into another source (e.g., your accounting system), pandas is an excellent choice. Pandas excels at ETL (Extract, Transform, Load) procedures. Some argue that many accountants are essentially ETL developers who may not be particularly skilled in their jobs so only use Excel.

FIRST DATAFRAME

Pandas DataFrame is the primary object used in pandas. It's similar to a virtual spreadsheet as it has rows and columns. When manipulating data, you'll often modify entire columns or iterate through each row.

Let's explore some sample data. To obtain this data, I opened a sample company file in Quickbooks Desktop and accessed the "Sales by Item Detail" report (Reports>Sales>Sales By Item Detail). This data will be included in the source material for this book, or you can pull similar data from any accounting system.

To import the data, you'll first need to install openpyxl. To do this, enter "pip install openpyxl" in the terminal.

Here is some code to create a pandas DataFrame from the Excel file. Save the code in the file "first_pandas_example.py".

```python
import pandas as pd

def main():
    df = pd.read_excel(
        r'C:\absolute_path_to_spreadsheet\QBD Sales By Item Detail.xlsx',
        'Sheet1'
    )
    print(df)

if __name__ == '__main__':
    main()
```

At this point, it might be challenging for you to visualize what the DataFrame looks like within the code. To better understand its structure, you can use PyCharm's Debugger. Place a breakpoint at the "print(df)" line and then run the Debugger. In the debugger window at the bottom of PyCharm, look at the right-hand window where you can see the "df" variable. Notice to the right of the variable, you'll see the words "View as DataFrame" in blue. See figure 13.1.

Figure 13.1

Click on "View as Dataframe". On the right hand side of Pycharm you'll notice a "SciView" window will open showing the data in the dataframe. See figure 13.2.

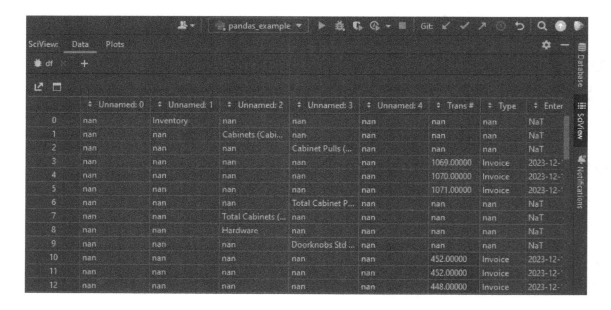

Figure 13.2

What you're looking at is the data as the code see's it. As you can imagine, this view will be extremely helpful as you're trying to edit the data in a meaningful way. As you make changes to the DataFrame you'll want to come back to this view and look at what it looks like after the changes. If you make the changes in the Debugger console you'll be able to see the changes in real time (although you may need to close the view and open it again after changes).

MANIPULATING THE DATAFRAME

We'll continue with the code we started with in the "First DataFrame" section. I'm going to provide a variety of examples on how to manipulate the DataFrame, but I'll present them in a way that allows you to apply them to various situations.

One crucial aspect to pay attention to is the DataFrame variable's location. For example, let's consider the code below:

```
df.drop(columns=['column_name']) #Won't work as expected
```

Although the above code removes the specified columns, it doesn't save the changes to the original DataFrame. Instead, it creates a copy of the DataFrame and waits for you to assign it somewhere. This might be confusing, but to correctly remove the columns and update the DataFrame, you should use the following code:

```
df = df.drop(columns=['column_name']) #Replace original variable
```

The updated code above creates a copy of the DataFrame with the columns removed and assigns it to the original variable. This is typically what you want to do unless you use the "inplace" argument, as shown below. The "inplace" argument is available in many DataFrame methods and allows you to modify the current DataFrame without creating a copy.

```
df.drop(columns=['column_name'], inplace=True) #Changes original Variable
```

Another argument to understand is the "axis" argument. The default value of the argument is 0, which refers to rows. If axis=1, it means columns. So, if you want to drop a column by the index, you would use the code below:

```
df.drop(df.columns[index], axis=1, inplace=True) #replace index with number
```

Again, I'm not attempting to provide an extensive Pandas tutorial here, but merely give you some basics. Below is some additional code that could help you use Pandas. I'll add this to the "first_pandas_example.py" file in Chapter 12's folder.

```
import pandas as pd

def remove_columns_examples(df):
    # df = df.drop(columns=['column_name'])
    # df.pop('column_name')
    # df.drop(columns=['column_name'], inplace=True)
```

```python
    # In below replace 'index' with number
    # df.drop(columns=df.columns[index], axis=1, inplace=True)
    # df.drop(columns=df.columns[:4], axis=1, inplace=True)
    df = df.dropna(axis=1, how='all') #Removes Columns if all rows NAN
    return df

def replace_nan_with_column_type(df):
    for col in df.columns:
        if df[col].dtype == 'float64' or df[col].dtype == 'int64':
            df[col].fillna(0, inplace=True)
        elif df[col].dtype == 'object':
            df[col].fillna("", inplace=True)
    return df

def convert_values(df):
    df['Date'] = pd.to_datetime(df['Date'])
    df['Trans #'] = df['Trans #'].round().astype(int)
    df['Ship Zip'] = df['Ship Zip'].round().astype(int).astype(str)

    return df

def select_row_by_value(df):
    df = df.loc[df['Date'] == '2024-12-14'] # filter by date
    df = df.loc[df['Type'] == 'Invoice'] #Filter Inovices
    #other operators like >, <, !=, etc. also work.

def iterate_through_rows(df):
    for i, row in df.iterrows():
        print(f'row index = {i}')
        print(f'row data = {row}')

def main():
    # Change the path in this file to match the absolute path
    # of your spreadsheet file.
    df = pd.read_excel(
     r'C:\absolute_path_to_spreadsheet\QBD Sales By Item Detail.xlsx',
        'Sheet1'
    )
    #Removes ROWS with NAN value in column
    df = df[pd.notnull(df['Trans #'])]
    df = remove_columns_examples(df)
    df = replace_nan_with_column_type(df)
    df = convert_values(df)
    print(df.shape[0]) # Row Count
    print(df.shape[1]) # Column Count
    select_row_by_value(df)

    print(df)

if __name__ == '__main__':
    main()
```

SECTION 4

API'S AND QUICKBOOKS

A Python for Accountants book would be incomplete without a section on QuickBooks. In this section, we'll primarily discuss connecting to QuickBooks Desktop and QuickBooks Online using various methods. We'll also cover API calls and how to consume and send JSON data. We'll start with API calls, as understanding them in Python is essential for making progress.

## CHAPTER 14

SyncFreedom And QBO

Instead of using generic trivia data like most tutorials, we'll train you with QuickBooks Online. First, you'll need to create an account with SyncFreedom.com. At the time of writing, you'll receive one free connection with your SyncFreedom.com account. Once you have the account, you'll want to connect to a QuickBooks Online account. If you have a QuickBooks Online Accountant login, you get one free QuickBooks Online Advanced subscription as your "Firm Books". We suggest using your firm books for testing. If you need further testing, you can also create a QuickBooks Online developer account, where you can set up additional sandbox company files to connect to.

WHY SYNCFREEDOM.COM

Most connectors to QuickBooks Online require you to go through their data interface. For example, if you're using an ODBC connector, you'll interface with QuickBooks data as if it's a typical database with tables. While this can be convenient, it's also restrictive. You're limited to the data they allow you access to, and if something's broken, you're waiting for the third party to fix it.

SyncFreedom allows you to interface directly with QuickBooks Online's API, giving you the freedom to access all available data without having to build an entire frontend web application. Furthermore, you'll be able to use all of the documentation that Intuit offers, instead of relying on third-party documentation that may lack critical details.

SYNCFREEDOM PACKAGE

To install SyncFreedom's library, go to the terminal and type in "pip install syncfreedom". Once installed, create a chapter14 folder and a file named config.ini inside the folder. Add the following information to config.ini. We also recommend adding the config.ini file to your .gitignore file to prevent it from accidentally being committed to your repository.

```
[SYNCFREEDOM_CREDENTIALS]
username=your_syncfreedom_username
password=your_syncfreedom_password

[ENVIRONMENT_INFO]
company_id=company_realm_id
```

```
environment=Production
sync_freedom_url=https://syncfreedom.com
```

You'll obtain your company_id/company_realm_id from SyncFreedom. Next, add a file named 'syncfreedom_basics.py' inside the chapter14 folder. We'll include the following code in this file, which retrieves all of the customers:

```python
import os
from configparser import ConfigParser
from syncfreedom.client import SyncFreedomQuickBooks
from quickbooks.objects.customer import Customer

config = ConfigParser()
#assuming the config.ini file is at the same file location as this file
config.read(os.path.join(os.path.dirname(__file__), 'config.ini'))

company_id = config['ENVIRONMENT_INFO']['company_id']
credentials = config['SYNCFREEDOM_CREDENTIALS']

def main():
    qb = SyncFreedomQuickBooks(
        company_id=company_id,
        credentials=credentials
    )
    customers = Customer.all(qb=qb)
    print(customers)

if __name__ == '__main__':
    main()
```

The SyncFreedom library manages the QuickBooks client for you. Without it, you would need to build a web application that can handle the OAuth 2.0 workflow. Building web applications comes with an even bigger learning curve than what you're learning here. However, as long as you're using SyncFreedom, you don't have to worry about creating a web application.

PYTHON-QUICKBOOKS PACKAGE

The Python package used in conjunction with SyncFreedom can be found here: https://pypi.org/project/python-quickbooks/

When you're using the python-quickbooks package, anywhere it calls for a "client" argument, you'll swap it out with SyncFreedom's client object named "SyncFreedomQuickbooks". Other than that, you can build your program like any other developer would (without the OAuth 2.0 hassles).

CHAPTER 15

API's

API stands for Application Programming Interface. They enable communication between different software systems. In Python, you can use the requests library to interact with various APIs and retrieve or send data.

REQUESTS

First, you will need to install requests. In Pycharm, open the terminal and type in "pip install requests". The code below is for demonstration purposes and doesn't actually work. You'll need to modify the code according to your specific situation. To retrieve data, you would make a GET request like below:

```
import requests

response = requests.get("https://api.example.com/endpoint")
data = response.json()
```

To send data, you would use a POST request like below. This adds data to the database. Again, this is just sample information, not something that will actually work.

```
import requests

data = {"name": "John", "age": 30}
response = requests.post("https://api.example.com/endpoint", json=data)
data = response.json()
```

Often, your requests require authorization. One of the simpler ways to authenticate is by using Bearer tokens. Below is some sample code to send requests with Bearer authorization.

```
import requests

# API endpoint
url = "https://api.example.com/data"

# API credentials
api_key = "my_secret_api_key"
```

137

```python
# headers with credentials
headers = {
    "Content-Type": "application/json",
    "Authorization": f"Bearer {api_key}"
}

# make a GET request to the API
response = requests.get(url, headers=headers)

#check to see if the response was an error or not.
if response.status_code == 200:
    print(response.json())
else:
    # print an error message
    print(f"Error: {response.status_code}")
```

ENDPOINTS

Typically in your code, you'll have a base URL and an endpoint. When you're looking through an API's documentation, you won't see "http" or the domain in most of it. Instead, you will find an endpoint that looks something like the example below:

```
GET /v3/company/<realmID>/query?query=<selectStatement>
```

The documentation assumes that you already know the base URL from the "get started" or the beginning part of the documentation. For example, the code above is for the QuickBooks Online API for creating an account (https://developer.intuit.com/app/developer/qbo/docs/api/accounting/all-entities/account). It's assuming you know the base URL is "https://quickbooks.api.intuit.com". If you want to make a request in Python, you'll need to concatenate the base URL and the endpoint. So the code should look something like this:

```python
import requests

base_url = "https://quickbooks.api.intuit.com"
realm_id = 5617864
sql_query = "select * from Account"
account_endpoint = f"/v3/company/{realm_id}/query?query={sql_query}"

# construct the full URL
url = base_url + account_endpoint
response = requests.get(url)
data = response.json()
```

You should modify the code to include best practices and proper authorization, but hopefully, you're grasping the main idea. At times, you may need to pass parameters into the request. The following example demonstrates how this might look if you were attempting to find a 25-year-old named John.

```
import requests

base_url = "https://api.example.com"
user_endpoint = "/users"
url = base_url + user_endpoint

# parameters to filter the data
params = {
    "name": "John",
    "age": 25,
    "sort_by": "name"
}

response = requests.get(url, params=params)
```

JSON

Python dictionaries and JSON data share similarities but are not identical. Frequently, you need to convert dictionaries to JSON format and vice versa. Below is some basic code to demonstrate converting a Python dictionary to JSON and back again.

```
import json

# create a Python dictionary
data = {
    "name": "John",
    "age": 25,
    "city": "New York"
}

# convert the dictionary to a JSON string
json_data = json.dumps(data)
print(type(json_data))
dict_data = json.loads(json_data)

print(type(data))
```

PAGINATION

Pagination occurs when the API you're working with sends only a portion of the data at a time. For instance, you might need to obtain a list of 107 accounts, but you'll have to do it through multiple requests. The following sample code demonstrates how to incorporate pagination. Keep in mind that this is just an example, and you'll need to consult the documentation of your specific API. Different APIs may have variations in how you determine if there is more data to be retrieved.

```python
import requests

def pagination_example():
    base_url = 'https://api.example.com'
    page_number = 1
    page_size = 10

    # Keep track of all the results returned by the API
    results = []
    done = False

    while not done:
        url = f'{base_url}/items?page={page_number}&per_page={page_size}'
        response = requests.get(url)

        # Check the status code of the response
        if response.status_code != 200:
            raise Exception('Error: API returned a non-200 status code')
        data = response.json()
        results.extend(data['items'])

        # Check if there are more pages to retrieve
        if 'next' in data['meta']:
            page_number += 1
        else:
            done = True

    return results

if __name__ == '__main__':
    results = pagination_example()
    print(results)
```

CHAPTER 16

QuickBooks Desktop

QuickBooks Desktop is a unique platform. You can interact with it using ODBC connectors if you prefer, but it's not necessary if you learn a few essential techniques. Fortunately, I've already created a package that enables direct interaction with QuickBooks Desktop. To do this, you'll need to understand a couple of concepts in this chapter.

32 BIT VS 64 BIT

Honestly, I tried to avoid explaining this, as it adds another layer of complexity. However, if you want to interact with QuickBooks Desktop's backend (without paying for a third-party connector), we need to address this.

For an extended period, QuickBooks Desktop SDK was 32-bit. In 2022, it finally switched to 64-bit. I suggest sticking to 32-bit in your program builds, as it will likely be supported for years and will be compatible with older versions. To interact with 32-bit, you'll need a 32-bit Python interpreter. I've discussed changing your interpreter in previous chapters, so I won't revisit that here. You can find out which version you have in your interpreter by running the Python code below.

```python
import struct
print(struct.calcsize("P") * 8, "bit")
```

If you want to use your program for just yourself and you're using Quickbooks 2022 or newer you don't need to switch to 32 bit.

QUICKBOOKS DESKTOP SDK

Once you've ensured you have the correct Python architecture (32-bit vs 64-bit), it's time to address obtaining QuickBooks Desktop's SDK (Software Development Kit). You'll need to download and install the SDK. The main website where you can acquire the SDK is:

https://developer.intuit.com/app/developer/qbdesktop/docs/get-started/download-and-install-the-sdk

Pay attention to the SDK version, as you'll need the version number later.

QBXML

You're likely familiar with HTML, but you may not have encountered much XML. If you were to consider the relationship between HTML and XML, XML would be the parent of HTML. XML is a data structure that allows you to create your own tags, whereas HTML has predefined tags you need to follow for the code to work. QBXML is QuickBooks' version of XML. It functions similarly, but with established tags you must use (akin to HTML's established tags).

Let's discuss the difference between a tag and an element for a moment. A tag is to an element what a book cover is to a book. An element starts with an opening tag, ends with a closing tag, and contains all of the data (pages) between the tags. A tag represents only the beginning and ending parts, while the element comprises the whole structure (beginning, data, end).

For example, the QBXML code snippet below, when sent to QuickBooks Desktop, retrieves data for all accounts in response.

```
<?xml version="1.0" encoding="utf-8"?>
<?qbxml version="13.0"?>
<QBXML>
    <QBXMLMsgsRq onError="continueOnError">
        <AccountQueryRq requestID="1"/>
    </QBXMLMsgsRq>
</QBXML>
```

Let's break down what we're seeing here. The first two lines are the declaration section. They identify the versions of XML and QBXML being used and specify that the text is encoded in UTF-8. You need these first two lines for anything sent to QuickBooks Desktop. XML usually starts with a root element, which has sub-elements (children) underneath it. In this case, you could consider the root element to be "QBXML". Underneath a root element, you would have sub-elements. Sub-elements start with an opening tag like "<ElementName>" and end with a closing tag like "</ElementName>", and they contain additional sub-elements.

Sometimes, you'll see an empty element that looks like "<ElementName />", which is both an opening and closing tag in the same element. In the example, "AccountQueryRq" serves as both an opening and closing tag.

The "requestID" part of the tag above is called an attribute. Don't get too hung up on using the same word "attribute" in XML as in Python. We are quite literally speaking different languages (XML, not Python). If you were to compare XML to Python, I would say an XML attribute is most similar to a Python argument. The "requestID" attribute is specified in QuickBooks' SDK (Software Development Kit). You need to sequence your requests, so you could theoretically send a request for all accounts and all customers in the same request. In the case of QBXMLMsgsRq (QBXML Message Request), we want the program to continue if there is an error, so we set onError="continueOnError".

XML IN PYTHON

I've found the lxml package is one of the easiest XML packages to work with in Python. You can install it using pip by running pip install lxml in the terminal. To create the XML code for an account request as shown in the previous example, you can use the following Python code. First, create a "Chapter16" folder, then place "xml_example.py" inside the folder. After that, put the code below inside "xml_example.py":

```python
from lxml import etree as et

def main():
    root = et.Element("QBXML")
    QBXMLMsgsRq = et.SubElement(
        root,
        "QBXMLMsgsRq",
        onError="continueOnError"
    )
    AccountQueryRq = et.Element('AccountQueryRq')
    AccountQueryRq.attrib['requestID'] = "1"
    QBXMLMsgsRq.insert(1, AccountQueryRq)

    # There are fancy ways to add the declaration but this is simple
    declaration = """<?xml version="1.0" encoding="utf-8"?> \
        <?qbxml version="13.0"?>"""
    full_request = declaration + et.tostring(root, encoding='unicode')
    print(full_request)

if __name__ == '__main__':
    main()
```

All we're doing here is creating the xml string. You would still need to send the string to QuickBooks to process the request.

QUICKBOOKS DESKTOP PYPI PACKAGE

To send your request and receive a response in Python, you'll need to work with QuickBooks Desktop's SDK. There are several nuances related to working with sessions and other aspects, but fortunately, I've created a Python package to handle all the complexity associated with it. You can install the package I created by running pip install quickbooks-desktop in your terminal. With that package, your code can be as simple as the example below to retrieve all of the accounts. Place the sample code inside "quickbooks_desktop_sample.py" under the "Chapter16" folder.

```python
from quickbooks_desktop.session_manager import SessionManager
from lxml import etree as et

def main():
    qb = SessionManager(SDK_version='13.0')
    rq_root = et.Element('AccountQueryRq')
    active_status = et.Element('ActiveStatus')
    active_status.text = '1'
    rq_root.insert(1, active_status) # 1 here is index number
```

```python
#send request
response = qb.send_xml(rq_root)

# parse the response
rs_root = et.fromstring(response)
QBXMLMsgsRs = rs_root.getchildren()[0]
AccountQueryRs = QBXMLMsgsRs.getchildren()[0]
list_of_accounts = AccountQueryRs.getchildren()
for account_root in list_of_accounts:
    for element in account_root:
        print(f"{element.tag} = {element.text}")
    #stop after the first account
    break

if __name__ == '__main__':
    main()
```

In the code above, I did take the long way into parsing the response. I did that for illustration purposes so you could walk through what's going on a little better.

SECTION 5

USER INTERFACE AND DEPLOYMENT

As you grow more proficient in using Python, it's important to consider how you can share your apps with others. Ultimately, you want to refine your products so they are not entirely dependent on you. While there will always be some dependence on you since you built the app and have the source code, it's best to be able to hand off your work to others as you move on. Creating a small UI is a good way to facilitate this handoff. This section focuses on making simple UIs and packaging your project for delivery to a client.

CHAPTER 17

Logging And Error Handling

LOGGING

I could have introduced logging at any point, really. I'm introducing it here because you absolutely want logging when creating a program that you don't plan on operating yourself. I'm not going to go into too much detail here since accountants would use logging just like any other programmer, and there are plenty of tutorials out there that can explain exactly what to do. It may seem daunting at first, but once you learn the basics, you can create a boilerplate logger that suits your needs.

I'm going to give you the code I use for logging setup and explain some things on how to use it. Create a new file named "logger_setup.py" and put the below code in it.

```python
import logging
import os
import datetime as dt

def start_logger():
    logger = logging.getLogger()
    logger.setLevel(logging.DEBUG)
    formatter = logging.Formatter(
        '%(asctime)s:%(filename)s:%(funcName)s:%(lineno)d:%(message)s'
    )

    # create file folder to add logging to
    user_folder = os.path.expanduser('~') # saves to user's folder
    env_folder = os.path.join(user_folder, '.name_of_program')
    today = dt.date.today().strftime('%Y_%m_%d')
    logger_file = os.path.join(env_folder, f'{today}_name_of_program.log')
    fh = logging.FileHandler(logger_file)
    fh.setLevel(logging.DEBUG)
    fh.setFormatter(formatter)
    logger.addHandler(fh)

    # creating a console handler so you can see the log inside of the UI
    ch = logging.StreamHandler()
    ch.setLevel(logging.DEBUG)
    ch.setFormatter(formatter)
    logger.addHandler(ch)
    return logger
```

After creating the logger file, you should add the following code to the top of your "main.py" file (where the program starts). Note that the logger variable is not created within the main function or any other function.

```
from Chapter17.logger_setup import start_logger

logger = start_logger()
```

Then, at the top of every page where you want to add logging, include the following code. Again, this code should not be inside any functions.

```
import logging

logger = logging.getLogger()
```

To print something to the actual log, use the following code. Replace the print function with this code wherever you want to log messages.

```
logger.debug("Any message you want to say")
```

The main purpose of the logger is to allow you to see what happened inside the code when you were not watching it. If someone calls you and says the program didn't work, you can ask them to grab the log and send it to you. With that in mind, you'll want to understand exactly what you're putting inside the log so you can troubleshoot it later.

Here are some ideas that can give you pseudo guidelines for logging. These are not sanctioned; they are just things I've done in the past that I've found helpful.

- Make the first and last line of a function/method a log. Indicate that you've successfully started and successfully ended the function. This is not required for every function, but you may want to add it to critical functions or ones you've already had problems with.
- Log a portion or all of the arguments passed in and/or data in your return statement. When there is an error, you can take the data you logged and add it to your tests. Then use Test Driven Development principles to fix the problem.
- Log the path chosen in if statements. This is similar to logging the first and last line of a function/method.
- Log the iteration number in loops. This will help you figure out which part of your data you need to look at for errors.
- Log inside your error handling.

ERROR HANDLING

Error handling can perform two different tasks for you. One task is to catch errors and take appropriate action depending on the type of error. Another task is to simplify your code. The keywords here are try and except. You instruct the code to try something, and if there is an error, you create an exception. See the example code below, which should be placed inside a file called "error_handling_examples.py" in the Chapter17 folder.

```python
def simple_handle():
    try:
        # You can't divide by zero
        result = 10 / 0
    except:
        print('this is an error')

def handle_with_unknown_exception():
    try:
        # You can't divide by zero
        result = 10 / 0
    except Exception as e:
        # This will print the type of error
        print("An error occurred:", e.__class__.__name__)

def handle_known_exception(num_1, num_2):
    try:
        # You can't divide by zero
        result = num_1 / num_2
    except ZeroDivisionError as e:
        # You know this error is possible
        print("I know you tried to divide by zero")
    except Exception as e:
        # To catch the unknown exception
        print("An error occurred:", e.__class__.__name__)
        raise("Whatever you did, it wasn't what I was expecting")


def main():
    simple_handle()
    handle_with_unknown_exception()
    handle_known_exception(10, 0)
    handle_known_exception(10, "I'm a string")

if __name__ == '__main__':
    main()
```

You can see in the "handle_known_exception" function that you can code to handle multiple types of errors depending on the desired response. Also, I used the raise function last because it stops the program in its tracks. If you were to edit "handle_with_unknown_exception" to raise an error, then "handle_known_exception" wouldn't run at all.

There is some controversy about when to use error handling. One argument says, if you're planning on errors, then extend your code for the different scenarios. In this case, error handling is a last resort. Another argument says you can't code for every exception, so sometimes error handling is the most straightforward way. There are good arguments for both, and I think the true answer lies somewhere in the middle.

One example is for user input. Let's say you're asking the user for a number. The longer and more proper way of ensuring it's a number would be to use a validator (to validate the type of the input) or an if statement. A simpler way is to just code what you want to do with the number and handle any errors that arise. The downside of the error handling method is that the error could be due to something else. So, you'll need to check the error type as well. See the example code below, which should be placed inside a file called "error_handling_examples_user_input.py":

```python
import easygui

def use_try():
    # with exception handling
    n = None
    while n is None:
        try:
            my_number = easygui.enterbox(
                title='Give Me A Number First Popup',
                msg="A number will pass, a string will make an error."
            )
            n = int(my_number)
            easygui.msgbox("Good Job! That was a number.")
        except ValueError:
            # if the code just gave a warning here that it wasn't
            #    a number it would.
            # cause a lot of confusion for the user if they passed a float.
            easygui.msgbox("That was not a number. Try again")

def use_if_without_try():
    # with checks
    n = None
    while n is None:
        my_number = easygui.enterbox(
            title='Give Me A Number Second Popup',
            msg="A number will pass a string will make an error."
        )
        if my_number.lstrip('-').isdigit():
            n = int(my_number)
            easygui.msgbox("Good Job! That was a number.")
        #Check if it was a float and round
        elif my_number.lstrip('-').split('.')[0].isdigit():
            n = int(float(my_number).__round__(0))
            easygui.msgbox("Good Job! That was a number.")
        else:
            easygui.msgbox(f"That was not a number. Try again")

def main():
    use_try()
    use_if_without_try()

if __name__ == '__main__':
    main()
```

In the example above, if the user inputs a float (e.g., 1.1), the error message would indicate that it's not a number. However, 1.1 is indeed a number, just not an integer. In such a situation, the user might struggle to understand the issue and could blame the developers. Although using the try-except block made the coding process easier, it is essential to provide clear error messages to avoid confusion. For instance, you could modify the message to clarify that a non-decimal integer is required. This example illustrates that there isn't always a clear right or wrong way to handle errors, as long as the code functions properly.

CHAPTER 18

Tkinter

Tkinter is a built-in Python library ideal for creating simple desktop applications. It's free and easy to use, making it a great starting point for beginners. While there are other tools and options available, such as web applications, they often have a steeper learning curve. The aim here is to provide a basic understanding of Tkinter so you can start exploring it on your own.

TKINTER VOCABULARY

To effectively build a user interface (UI) with Tkinter, it's essential to understand the basic terminology used in its documentation.

- Root — The "Toplevel" widget of Tkinter; everything goes into the root. It's like an open box where you put things inside. In PowerPoint terms, the root is the "Send To Back" object. The Python object is "tkinter.Tk". The root.title is your program's name.
- PanedWindow — A container (smaller box) that holds subwindows. Usually, there's a "main_pane" that is the same size as your root/overlays on your root. Everything goes into the main_pane except for the menu (file, edit, help, etc.).
- Labelframe — It's the frame that actually acts like a frame (something that goes around another thing). It goes around an area and you can put some text on top of it.
- Entry — An input box where you can type into.
- Button — It's a button. You click it and it triggers stuff.
- Calendar — A calendar where you can select dates. I haven't had a lot of luck with Calendar.
- Grid — There are a few ways to structure your application, I'm going to tell you to stick with a grid pattern. The grid pattern is like a table with columns and rows. The default column is 0 and the default row is the next available row (starts with 0). You define how many columns and rows. There are also nested columns and rows inside defined cells (cells isn't the technical term). So the area 0, 1 could have a 4 X 5 grid inside of it.
- Sticky — Sometimes we'll create widgets that are smaller than the area of our cell. For example a button with minimal text will only be a little bigger than the text. If we want it to stretch all the way across the column and row we use the sticky parameter to stick it to whatever side we want (N, S, E, and W).
    - Stick to north and south side: sticky=N+S
    - Stick to west and east side: sticky=W+E
    - Stick to all sides: sticky=NW+SE (specifying corners to stick to instead of sides)

- Columnspan and Rowspan. Using the "columnspan" and "rowspan" parameters you can make merge (merge isn't the technical term is the excel term) a cell across multiple columns or rows.
  - Stretch across two columns: columnspan=2
  - Stretch across three rows: rowspan=3

TKINTER FIRST PROGRAM

In this first program, we are going to create a fairly simple application that is commonly used for tasks such as importing an Excel sheet into QuickBooks, manipulating the data in the sheet, and more. The program will consist of two halves. The left half will have two buttons: one for selecting a file and the other for performing an action with the file. The right half will have a field displaying the file location string and, below that, a small instructions area. When completed, the program will look similar to Figure 18.1.

Figure 18.1

I'm going to start with some boilerplate code you can see below.

```python
import os
import sys
import signal
from tkinter import ttk, Label, Entry, Button, filedialog, messagebox
import tkinter as tk

class App:

    def __init__(self, root):
        self.root = root

        # Right here is where all our code will go

        #different ways to kill the program.
        #I suggest leaving all of these ways here.
        self.root.protocol('WM_DELETE_WINDOW', self.quit)
        self.root.bind('<Control-q>', self.quit)
        signal.signal(signal.SIGINT, self.quit)


    def quit(self, *args):
        self.root.quit()
        self.root.destroy()
        sys.exit()

def main():
    root = tk.Tk()
```

```
    root.title('my_program_name')
    app = App(root)
    app.root.mainloop()

if __name__ == '__main__':
    main()
```

First, create the root by instantiating the "tkinter.Tk" class. Then, give the instance the title of the program using the title method.

Next, we will create an instance of the App class, which is our custom class. When creating the instance, we will attach the root using a composition object-oriented approach (recall composition from earlier in the book). Additionally, we will add the boilerplate quit method and ways to quit when called. You don't need to have an extensive understanding of how it quits; simply copy the code provided.

To continue building the UI within the __init__ method, we'll first create a main window to place everything inside. We'll create the main pane using the following code:

```
self.main_pane = ttk.PanedWindow(self.root, orient='vertical')
self.main_pane.grid(sticky='nsew') #Column and Row are Default to 0
```

In the first line, we create a PanedWindow instance and specify that the window should be placed within the root. The second line sets the size of the main pane to be the same as the root and makes it stick to all sides of the root.

Now, we'll go ahead and split the main pane into two halves (a left and right side).

```
# splitting the program into a left and right side
self.left_vertical_pane = ttk.PanedWindow(
    self.main_pane,
    orient='vertical'
)
self.left_vertical_pane.grid(column=0, row=0, sticky='nsew')

self.right_vertical_pane = ttk.PanedWindow(
    self.main_pane,
    orient='vertical'
)
self.right_vertical_pane.grid(column=1, row=0, sticky='nsew')
```

Notice the column and row in the grid function. The "left_vertical_pane" is in column zero and the "right_vertical_pane" is in column one. This will allow us to put the buttons and the input side by side. Now let's put the two buttons on the left side, one on top of the other.

```
#putting 2 buttons on the left side
select_file_btn = Button(
    self.left_vertical_pane,
    text='Select File',
```

```
        command=self.select_file
    )
    select_file_btn.grid(row=0, sticky='nsew')

    select_file_btn = Button(
        self.left_vertical_pane,
        text='Do Something',
        command=self.do_something
    )
    select_file_btn.grid(row=1, sticky='nsew')
```

In this example, the column defaults to zero (o), so we only need to specify the row. The first button is placed in row o and the second button in row 1. Each button is associated with a method that we haven't created yet. We'll define these methods within the "App" class, below the __init__ method. Before that, let's complete the right side of the UI. On the right side, we want an entry field where users can paste the desired file path. Additionally, we want a label to display basic instructions below the entry field. We'll add the remaining lines of code to the __init__ method, placing the "kill" codes after this part.

```
    # putting an input field on the right side
    self.file_input_box = Entry(self.right_vertical_pane)
    self.file_input_box.grid(row=0, sticky='we')

    #putting a label under the input field
    self.instructions = Label(
        self.right_vertical_pane,
        text='Click On Do Something After Selecting A File'
    )
    self.instructions.grid(row=1)
```

Just like the buttons, I'm specifying the two objects in their respective rows. I'm also adding the first argument as the right pane vs. the left pane.

Now in between the kill lines and the quit method let's add the below code to select a file.

```
    def select_file(self):
        filetypes = (
            ('Excel files', '*.xlsx*'),
        )
        selection = filedialog.askopenfilename(
            title='Select File Dialog',
            initialdir=os.path.expanduser('~'),
            filetypes=filetypes
        )
        self.__setattr__('file_selected', selection)
        self.file_input_box.delete(0, len(self.file_input_box.get()))
        self.file_input_box.insert(0, self.file_selected)
```

When the user clicks the "Select File" button, the askopenfilename method will open a file selection dialog in the user's folder ('~'), filtering for Excel files. If you want to allow any file type, you can use "*" as the filter. After the user selects a file, the file path is assigned to the selection variable. We then use the __setattr__ method to set the file_selected attribute of the App class. The file_input_box delete and insert methods are utilized to replace any existing content in the file_input_box with the newly selected file location.

For the do_something method, we'll include some placeholder code. You can replace this code with the desired functionality for the selected Excel sheet (or any other file type).

```python
def do_something(self):
    if hasattr(self, 'file_selected'):
        messagebox.showinfo(
            'title',
            f'I did something with the file name "{self.file_selected.
split("/")[-1]}"'
        )
    else:
        messagebox.showinfo('title', 'You need to select a file first')
```

If you want to modify the code to select a folder I would swap out "askopenfilename" for the "askdirectory" method.

You can find the complete code in the "Chapter18" folder "first_tkinter.py" file.

DRAG AND DROP GUI BUILDERS

There are several GUI builders available that you could potentially use. I have explored various options, including both desktop and web-based GUI tools. After learning and trying to integrate these tools into my development process, I've come to the following conclusion: Drag-and-drop builders are more suitable for dedicated UI designers and developers. However, the learning curve for each tool is often longer than it takes to learn the straightforward Tkinter library. Documentation might be inadequate, and you may find yourself struggling to get things to work. Once you manage to make it work, you might realize that you could have spent less time coding everything by hand.

Can you become faster with drag-and-drop builders? Probably... eventually. But unless you commit to becoming a dedicated developer with a single tool or environment, the time invested might not be worthwhile. Knowledge gained in one tool has limited transferability to another. It's not like learning Excel makes you proficient in Google Sheets. GUI tools may share core concepts, but in practice, they can be as different as QuickBooks and NetSuite.

I suggest learning the fundamentals and basics of designing a Tkinter app through code alone. You don't need to know everything, just a solid understanding of the essentials. The learning curve isn't steep, and once you grasp it, you can quickly create simple apps without additional complications. Keeping it simple is often the best approach for most projects.

If you still want to explore other options, some starting points include Anvil.works for web apps and Pygubu for desktop apps. Proceed at your own risk. While these tools can be useful if you're already a developer in the underlying technology, they might not be great for learning transferable skills. For example, being proficient in Anvil.works won't necessarily make you a skilled web developer. Consider yourself cautioned.

## CHAPTER 19

Deployment

There are several effective ways to deploy your code. While you could always run your code in PyCharm each time you need it, this approach can become tedious. In this guide, I'll share a few successful deployment strategies I've come across.

REQUIREMENTS.TXT

The first thing you need to understand and create is the "requirements.txt" file. Regardless of your deployment method, it's essential to know what this document is and how to generate it. The file lists the packages your project requires, along with their installed versions. When using a git repository, you typically don't want to include your virtual environment. So, when you download the project onto another computer, how can you recreate the same environment you used for development? The answer lies in the requirements.txt file, which contains a list of all the packages and their corresponding versions used during development.

To create the file, open the terminal in PyCharm with your virtual environment activated. You'll know your virtual environment is active when you see "(venv)" on the left side of "PS C:\absolute_path_to_your_project>" in your terminal. If it doesn't display "venv," it's because you named your virtual environment differently. In this case, the actual name would appear as "(your_environment_name)."

Inside your terminal you'll run the below command.

```
pip freeze > requirements.txt
```

This will create the document in your project's top directory.

PYINSTALLER

My preferred package for creating an executable is PyInstaller. An executable is a file with the ".exe" extension. These unique files contain everything required to run the program you've developed. To install PyInstaller, you first need to execute the following command in the terminal to install the package.

```
pip install pyinstaller
```

Figure 19.1

The subsequent command you'll need to run includes some optional arguments. You can add these arguments to the command using a double dash (--) followed by the argument. Below, I've provided the command I use with my preferred arguments, which you can modify to suit your needs. The primary argument you should always include is "--onefile", which consolidates everything into a single transferable exe file. "--windowed" is highly recommended but not strictly necessary in every situation. "--icon" allows you to add an icon to the executable.

```
pyinstaller --onefile --icon=icon_file_name.ico --windowed main.py
```

After the executable has been created, you can rename the file to your desired name. To transport the executable, you'll want to compress it into a folder. Avoid attaching an executable file to an email without first compressing it into a zipped folder. Once the product has been delivered, the user can simply double-click on the executable file to run it.

AUTOMATED SCRIPTS

Creating scripts that run automatically is a powerful feature. In this tutorial, I'll explain how to run a Python script in a Windows environment at a specific time every day. You can modify the instructions to suit your needs, but some steps must be followed precisely.

Windows Task Scheduler is built into every Windows machine, so you can open it from the Start menu by typing "Windows Task Scheduler." Once it's open, we'll want to create a new folder for our scripts to keep things organized. Right-click on the folder named "Task Scheduler Library" and select "New Folder...". See figure 19.1.

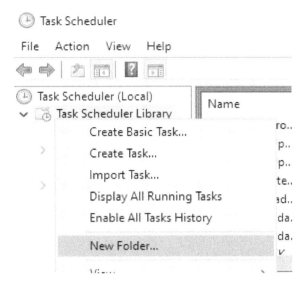

Figure 19.1

We will name the new folder "AccountingPyTasks"; however, you can choose any name you like. It's essential not to modify existing tasks or folders, as this could cause issues with your computer. That's why we're creating a dedicated folder for our tasks.

Before running a script, we need to create one. From my experience, simpler scripts are more likely to run successfully. Complex scripts that involve opening browsers and other tasks can be challenging to make work consistently. For this example, we'll place the following code in the "Chapter19" folder in a file named "script_to_run_automatically.py".

```
import easygui
easygui.msgbox("It worked!")
```

As mentioned, we're keeping things simple. After you have your script (code in a ".py" file) created, open Task Scheduler. Click on the folder you created earlier. In the menu bar, click on "Action" and then "Create Task" (not "Create Basic Task"). In the "General" tab, give the task a name. I named mine "run_automated_task". Inside the "Security options," you can choose to run only when logged on or regardless. The checkbox next to "Run with the highest privileges" is similar to starting a program on your computer using the "Run as administrator".

For now, select "Run only when the user is logged on." Then change "Configure for:" at the bottom to your Windows operating system or one below. I'm choosing Windows 10. See figure 19.2.

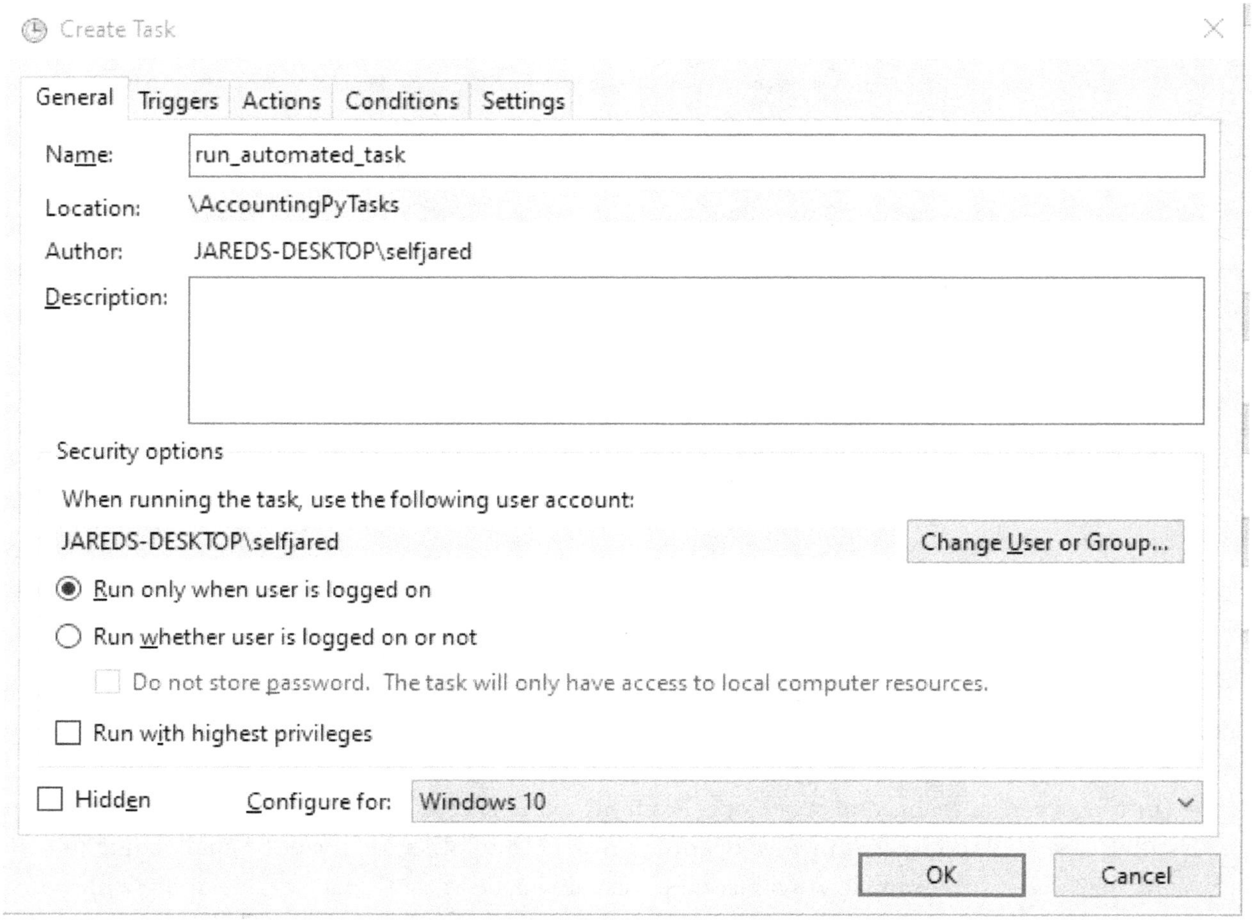

Figure 19.2

Now, move to the "Triggers" tab and select "New...". You can see that there are quite a few options you can choose from. For the sake of testing, we're going to set our settings to work "On a schedule," "One time," and choose a time a couple of minutes in the future. See figure 19.3.

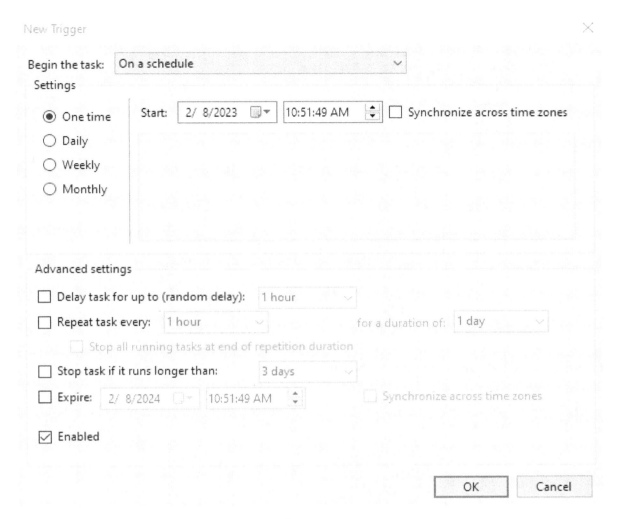

Figure 19.3

Click "Ok" and then go to the "Actions" tab and select "New...". Now, it is crucial to get this part right. In the "Program/script:" box, enter the absolute path to the Python executable in your virtual environment. In my case, it's "C:\Users\selfjared\Documents\PythonProjects\AccountingPy\venv\Scripts\python.exe". Add the path inside the box without any quotation marks.

In the "Add arguments (optional):" box, add the absolute path to the script you want to run, again without any quotation marks. In my case, it's "C:\Users\selfjared\Documents\PythonProjects\AccountingPy\Chapter19\ script_to_run_automatically.py".

In the "Start in (optional):" box, add the absolute path to the virtual environment folder, without quotation marks. In my case, it's "C:\Users\selfjared\Documents\PythonProjects\AccountingPy\venv". See figure 19.4.

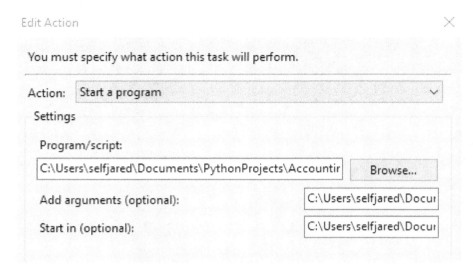

Figure 19.4

Once you've filled everything out, click OK to close the "Edit Action" window, and then click OK again to close the "Create Task" window. At this point, the trigger time might be in the past, so ensure that it's set for the future. If you need to edit anything, double-click on the task in the "Task Scheduler" window.

Now, if you wait for your computer's time to match the time of the task, your program should run as scheduled. Alternatively, you can run it manually by right-clicking on the task and selecting "Run". See figure 19.5.

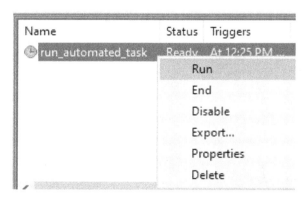

Figure 19.5

When it runs you will get the popup saying it worked. Notice that a command window will also pop up. I've tried various methods to keep the command window from coming up but haven't found a successful way to do it yet. If you have one that you tested and you know works, shoot me an email so I can update this section with it.

Here are some interesting settings you may want to consider:

- General > Security Options > Run whether user is logged on or not: Although this feature could be useful, running more complex programs can be challenging. For example, if you want to scrape a website at 2 am every morning, it might fail due to various permission levels that need to be set correctly. Getting your computer to that point is beyond the scope of this book, which is why I almost left this section out entirely, as I've faced many issues automating tasks using this feature.

- Conditions > Power > Wake the computer to run this task: This setting could be helpful when paired with running tasks when the user is not logged on. However, it is only one of many settings that need to be perfect for a script to run unsupervised. Be aware that setting up the ideal environment for such tasks can be a complex process.

- General > Security Options > Run with highest privileges: This option is similar to right-clicking on a program and selecting "Run as administrator." However, using this setting may cause more problems than it solves, so it's recommended to leave it unselected unless you have a specific reason to run the task with elevated privileges.

- Triggers > New… > Begin the task > At log on: This is an interesting trigger option. It allows you to set a task to run automatically when you log in to your computer. This can be quite useful in scenarios where you want to initiate the script execution as soon as you arrive at work and log in, allowing the script to run while you get settled in for the day.

- Triggers > New… > Begin the task > On an event: This trigger option offers many interesting possibilities since it allows you to initiate a script based on specific events occurring on your system. However, the range of options is quite extensive, and it might take some exploration to find the most suitable event to trigger your script. For example, you could consider triggering a script every time you log in to a QuickBooks file or some other application. If you discover an innovative use case or event to trigger your script, shoot me an email!

- Settings > If the task fails, restart every: While this setting might seem helpful in certain situations, it could also be potentially dangerous. The last thing you want is to create an endless loop that constantly attempts to restart a failed task, which could significantly slow down or even crash your computer. It's essential to use this setting with caution and consider other ways to handle failed tasks, such as error logging and notifications, to address the issue more efficiently.

- Settings > Stop the task if it runs longer than: It's a good idea to set this option to a reasonable duration, based on how long the task typically takes to run when supervised. As a rule of thumb, you can set it to at least twice the maximum time the task usually takes. For instance, if the task takes less than 30 minutes to run, set the limit to an hour. If it takes 35 minutes, set it to 2 hours. It's important not to set the limit too high, as excessively long durations, such as days, may not be practical and could lead to issues.

- Settings>If the task is already running, then the following rule applies:
  - Do not start a new instance: This is the safest setting, as it prevents new instances from starting if the task is already running, likely due to a failed run that never stopped.
  - Run a new instance in parallel: Selecting this option could lead to issues, as it may spin up multiple instances. It's not advisable to choose this unless you have a good understanding of multithreading and how to manage it.
  - Queue a new instance: This could be helpful if your trigger isn't based on a clock, such as an event trigger. However, in most other cases, it's not recommended.
  - Stop the existing instance: While this may seem like a popular option, it's important to remember that if the script didn't work the first time, it's unlikely to work the second time without intervention and changes.

SECTION 6

CHAT GPT

Chat GPT became famous at about the time I was finishing this book. As I went through the editing phase of this book it became clear that I needed to include a section on this topic. I use Chat GPT often to help me. It's improved the speed of development for a number of projects. To be honest, it can only help with small tasks. You need to give the prompt correct vocabulary to really get meaningful code out of it. I would use it as an assistant. That said, the assistant isn't in charge, you are. So take control of Chat GPT don't let it control you. Learn the principles of programming then ask Chat GPT to do the leg work.

CHAPTER 20

Writing Good Prompts

Chat GPT will write good code but won't write good programs. It doesn't have a really long memory and can forget what you told it to do. Because of this you want to piece things out in a small way that can all be handled in a small response. This goes back to the principle of writing small manageable functions instead of really big complex functions.

For example, if you write a prompt that says "write me an accounting program in Python" it's going to tell you no. Instead, you may want to ask for steps or things to consider like "Give me the essential parts of an accounting program." That should give you a response that says you need a chart of accounts. Then ask "Give me the code for a chart of accounts." This will actually give you an output of code that makes some sense.

Even though Chat GPT might give you a piece of the puzzle in your program, it's your responsibility to put the puzzle together. Let's come back to the chart of accounts example. With all of the knowledge you gained in this book let's ask Chat GPT to actually do some meaningful things. Try these prompts which I used to create a simple program:

- Create a python class called "Account". Give the class the attributes id, number, name, account_type, and description. Add a method that can add the account to an sqlite database table with the same name as the class. The name of the database will be "my_accounting.db." Add a method to get the account from the database by searching for the account number, name, or id. Add a delete method that will delete the account. Make sure no accounts can have the same name.
- Create a tkinter ui that has two tabs. One tab has fields that can be filled out for the Account class you just gave me. Also have a save button that calls the add_to_database method in the Account class. Have the second tab in the ui be a list of the accounts retrieved from the sqlite database. On the right of each row have a delete button. When the delete button is clicked have the account in that row be deleted using the delete_account method. Don't give me the account class I only the the code for tkinter.
- Give me the code to start AccountUI.
- In the AccountsUI class under the load_accounts method you reference the method Accounts.get_accounts(). Give me the method.
- Give me the code to make sure the database is created.

Note: Sometimes responses can't be contained in a single prompt. So you just tell Chat GPT to continue where it left off. If the code stops in the delete_account method, say "continue the code from delete_account".

I added the program into this chapter's support material. The thing to note about the program is it doesn't all work. I intentionally left it that way. The point is Chat GPT will give you a lot of the pieces but it doesn't always create working code. You need to take what Chat GPT gives you and then create a program that works. You can only do that by understanding the other principles and lessons in this book.

Conclusion

Congratulations on completing this book! There is so much more to learn about Python, so don't stop learning. Some great resources to start with include Google, YouTube, and ChatGPT. If you've made it this far and would like to provide feedback, I'd love to hear it! This book has the potential to evolve into a living resource with regular updates as more accountants embark on this journey. Together, we can explore how to adopt Python as the go-to language for accountants.

www.ingramcontent.com/pod-product-compliance
Lightning Source LLC
LaVergne TN
LVHW081658050326
832903LV00026B/1807